it's *your* **move!**

An inclusive approach to dance

peppy hills

The *Questions Publishing Company* **Ltd** Birmingham 2003

The Questions Publishing Company Ltd
321 Bradford Street, Digbeth, Birmingham B5 6ET

First published in 2003

ISBN: 1 84190 097 4

Written by: Peppy Hills
Photography by: Amanda Greenley, Josie Bourne, Peppy Hills, Cae Hayes, Merie Hope, Esther
                 Sayers, Mike Fletcher, Mike Eglesfield
Edited by: Katherine Pate
                 Amanda Greenley
Designed by: James Davies

Printed in the UK

Acknowledgements
Cae Hayes for her time and invaluable advice
Caroline Scott and Wild Ducks
Louise Glynn
Angie Cardwell (Advisory Teacher for Psychological Services, City of Birmingham Education Department)
Wilson Stuart School, especially their Physiotherapy Department, Birmingham
Welcombe Hills School, Warwickshire
Calthorpe School and Sports College, Birmingham
Centre for Arts Therapy, Timisoara, Romania
James Brindley School, Birmingham
Frontline Dance Company
Sunfield, Worcestershire

Contents

Introduction

Dancing can be an exciting, enjoyable experience for all. It enables you to feel different, to be different and to create movements and dance pieces that you had no idea were lurking within your mind and body.

In the past decade, dance has been introduced in a large number of special schools, day centres, hospitals and numerous places other than mainstream schools and youth clubs. There are dance companies whose members are not the stereotypical type of dancer with a specific shape and way of moving, but dancers who use wheelchairs, who are deaf, who have learning disabilities. Nowadays, dance participants are an ever increasing population with increasingly diverse needs.

It is challenging to lead dance sessions with groups of people who have a wide range of learning styles and different ways of accessing dance material. All dance work should be of high quality, accessible and inclusive, and the pressure is on teachers, dance practitioners and dance artists to develop and deliver this.

When I first began working with an increasingly wide range of participants, at times I felt bewildered and confused. Initially I had little experience in this area, but over the past fifteen years I have gained knowledge and confidence and developed approaches that I wish I had known about in the beginning. This book presents this way of working, which is accessible to participants of all abilities.

It's your move! highlights:
➤ issues that dance leaders need to be aware of, e.g. health and safety;
➤ pointers to developing creative and accessible ways of working;
➤ questions to help you evaluate your own dance practice and delivery;
➤ examples of tried and tested dance work.

It's your move! is for anyone involved in delivering dance in any setting, particularly those working with people with diverse needs and disabilities. The term 'disability' covers an enormous range of conditions. This book does not consider them individually, but presents ways of working that can be adapted to dancers with different needs. In addition, there are chapters on working with specific groups, such as 'dancers with high energy' and 'dancers with limited movement'.

This is the book I wish I had had fifteen years ago!

Peppy Hills

Practical and logistical points to remember

➤ *Seek advice from physio/medical staff and teaching staff* prior to sessions (and during sessions if necessary). Check whether activities are outside a dancer's normal range of movement, e.g. working on the floor, out of a chair. Ensure that you are aware of dancers' individual physical management programmes.

➤ *Ensure that you are aware of dancers' particular medical conditions* that could affect their:
  ➤ range of movement,
  ➤ stamina,
  ➤ comfort,
  (e.g. brittle bones, epilepsy, osteoporosis).

➤ *You will need to build a diverse range of resources* to use during sessions, including:
  ➤ music/sounds
  ➤ videos
  ➤ pictures and other visual stimuli
  ➤ props and objects
  Ensure your collection includes a range of styles and cultural influences. This can be a mission of a lifetime – enjoy collecting!

➤ *Ensure that you have had the appropriate checks,* e.g. CRB and police checks, that enable you to work with groups of young people.

➤ *Be aware of your time management* during a session. Allow sufficient time for dancers to:
  ➤ move from task to task (e.g. getting from standing to sitting will take different amounts of time for different people, you may need specialist equipment);
  ➤ process and understand instructions – particularly if interpretation is involved;
  ➤ explore ideas;
  ➤ articulate and present responses, both verbal and non-verbal.

➤ *Ensure that you have a suitable support worker to dancer ratio* in the dance session. You may need to run staff training prior to dance sessions, to clarify support workers' roles and the ways of working within a dance session.

➤ *Ensure that staff working within your session are aware and responsible for their own health and safety.*
Check that:
  ➤ support staff are aware of what is physically required within a session, e.g. floor work, and can assess their own health and safety;
  ➤ staff are aware of their own bodies and are able to rest when needed during a session, e.g. after long periods of supporting a student on the floor, or standing.
  You may need to address these issues in staff training prior to dance sessions.

➤ *Seek advice on using any specialist equipment* within a session, e.g. hoists for lifting. Only use equipment with the sanction of physio/medical or teaching staff.
Check:
  ➤ the availability of equipment for a session;
  ➤ that whoever is operating the equipment is trained and qualified to do so;
  ➤ that you have planned a realistic amount of time for using equipment within your session. It may be more time consuming that you realise.

➤ *Ensure that you are familiar with the institution's policies* on:
  ➤ behaviour management,
  ➤ physical management,
  ➤ student confidentiality.
Individual students may have specific programmes.

➤ *All communication and requests should go through your initial point of contact* within the school/institution, e.g. class teacher. It is important that he/she is fully informed of all developments.

➤ *You will need adequate Public Liability Insurance* if you are working as a freelance artist or practitioner in a school/institution. You are responsible for getting yourself insured.

4

➤ *You will need permission to take photographs of or film participants in your sessions.* Most schools and institutions have a generic letter asking whether a child's/young adult's photograph may be taken for use in school/educational settings. Parents/guardians/carers then give written consent, or not. Permission is reviewed and often revoked by Social Services if the child/adult is under their remit for any reason.

You must check procedures for permissions with the organisations and institutions you are working in.

Important!

➤ *Make sure that **you** still have opportunities to dance.* Your enjoyment of dance will be infectious!

Small dances — big value

Working with dancers with limited movement

All too often, people who are unable to move their own limbs independently, or who lack control of their movements, are seen as being 'un-physical'. Consequently they may not be included in physical experiences such as dance. For anyone who has a fixed view of what a dancer looks like (e.g. able bodied, perfect proportions, technically very able) the notion of someone with severe disabilities dancing can be extremely challenging.

Once, during a telephone call to a day centre to organise a series of dance/movement sessions (negotiated by a local arts officer), the deputy manager of the centre responded by saying "Oh no, you won't want to work with our clients, they don't dance, they are handicapped". Hence access to such activities can be denied before any individual is given the opportunity to experience it and decide for him or herself.

'Dancers with limited movement' includes people with a wide range of specific individual conditions and combinations of conditions, including those with severe physical disabilities and/or sensory impairments, with and without moderate to severe learning difficulties. This definition may also include people who are quadriplegic, those with severe cerebral palsy and those with degenerative conditions such as muscular dystrophy.

1

7

Starting point

A crucial starting point is to work with the dancers as they are – here and now, and to explore all possibilities. In this way you *focus on abilities and possibilities.* This is the key to positive and creative sessions, as opposed to working towards how a dancer's body 'should' be.

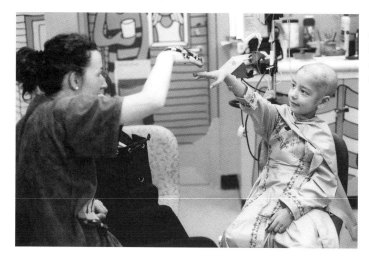

Focusing on what *is* possible is the key to positive and creative sessions

Practical and logistical issues

Often the most effective work is produced when the dancer to support worker ratio is 1:1. This obviously has staffing implications, and also means support workers need to be clear about:

➤ their role within the sessions,

➤ the aims of the session,

➤ ways of working,

➤ health and safety issues (see *Practical and logistical points to remember* on page 3),

➤ the physical/emotional needs of the dancer with whom they are working.

Preparation

The size of the group can often depend on the space and staffing available. Whilst a session can consist of one child and one support worker working alone, it is important to remember that *dance can be a session where individuals who are normally quite isolated can be part of a group activity, and be pro-active.*

Dance can be a session where individuals who are normally quite isolated can be part of a group activity, and be pro-active

Practical preparations for sessions include leaving plenty of time for:

➤ students to have refreshments (ensuring they are well hydrated),

1

8

➤ visiting the bathroom,

➤ getting in and out of chairs and other equipment as appropriate.

Comfort and safety

The comfort of all participants is a key concern in all dance sessions. If dancers are coming out of their wheelchairs or other equipment and working on the floor, equipment such as mats, cushions and beanbags may be needed to ensure all students and support staff are safe and comfortable.

Partnership

The relationship between dancer and support worker is crucial. During sessions it is imperative that able-bodied assistants do not take over and 'do movement to the dancer'. Support workers are there to facilitate the dancer's movements and to dance with them. The support worker may need to give input at times, but this needs to be done sensitively and without taking over. The working relationship needs to be two-way, with the support worker listening, watching, feeling and taking cues – visual, oral and physical – from the dancer, allowing the dancer to indicate choices and initiate movements.

The working relationship needs to be two-way, with the support worker listening, watching, feeling and taking cues from the dancer

Support workers should facilitate the dancer's movements

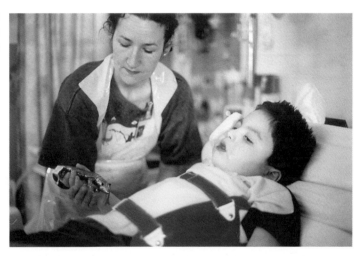

Support workers need to develop the ability to:
➤ listen, watch and feel for cues, nuances and responses from the student,
➤ adapt,
➤ improvise,
➤ translate,

1

9

- ➤ follow a dancer's movements,
- ➤ enjoy moving with another person,
- ➤ be comfortable working on the floor (as required).

A successful partnership is rewarding for both parties. Dancers and support workers must be given time to get to know each other, and to get used to working together. Hence it may be advisable for support workers and dancers to work in the same partnership for a minimum of half a term. However, if a partnership is not succeeding it can become restrictive, uncomfortable and possibly unworkable. Such issues need to be addressed and remedied in order for the dancer and support worker to have a positive experience of dance.

Staff training issues

You may need one or more staff training sessions in preparation for 1:1 work with dancers with limited movement. Any additional staff brought in for dance sessions should also attend the training.

Training sessions could explore:
- ➤ being comfortable working on the floor,
- ➤ moving together with others,
- ➤ physically experiencing different movements and sequences (rolling, stretching, pushing),
- ➤ qualities of touch and close contact work, e.g. use of massage,
- ➤ body awareness,
- ➤ physically listening to another person (breathing patterns, tension in their body, feeling movements they initiate),
- ➤ listening and feeling for cues from their partner,
- ➤ health and safety issues for staff and students (lifting, use of hoists, etc. See *Practical and logistical points to remember* on page 3).

Ways of maximising movement

Throughout the session it is important that the tasks given are 'open' and accessible to everyone in the group.

> **Example**
> Keeping two body parts together (foot to foot, palm to knee), see where you can move. How high can you move and how low? Can you make patterns in the air, such as zigzags and circles? What different speeds and directions can your movements take? This task does not exclude anyone as any body parts can be joined, and the smallest movement counts.

1

Total communication

During sessions it is important to keep all levels of communication open, such as spoken words, visual movements, touch, sounds and images (spoken or pictures). We all learn in different ways and it is important to include as many potential 'ways in' for dancers and support workers as possible.

Dance sessions could include:
- a continual verbal description of the movements that are happening,
- sounds/music (using voice or instruments) that compound the movement dynamic,
- singing/chanting,
- toys or gadgets that illustrate a particular movement, e.g. elastic stretching, jerky movements from a clockwork or automated toy,
- physical movements and demonstrations.

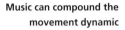
Music can compound the movement dynamic

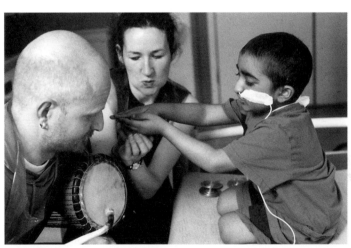

Be aware that dancers who have similar disabilities may show a preference for particular learning strategies.

> *Example*
> One of my colleagues has found that young people with a certain level of cerebral palsy find it easier to understand instructions when the teacher's voice echoes and illustrates the nature, dynamics and speed of a movement. For example, giving the instruction "we move up, up, up, s-l-o-w-l-y", raising the pitch on the "up, up" and slowing the voice for "slowly", as the dancers move, supports their movement and maximises their experience and understanding.

1

Time to experience and explore

It is crucial that sufficient time is allowed for participants to explore and experience movements. Some dancer/support staff partnerships will need time to repeat movements. Others will need time to work slowly towards completing a movement once. *All the participants must be allowed time to achieve.*

Physical support and assistance

At times it will be appropriate for the support worker physically to support and assist a dancer's movement. Make sure you and they are aware of any health and safety issues (see *Practical and logistical points to remember* on page 3). There may be a choice of ways in which you can assist movement. Safety, comfort and a minimal amount of 'doing movement to' the dancer, are sound guidelines.

> **Example**
> If you are assisting a dancer in moving their arms, you have a choice of putting your arm under theirs (with their arm lying on top of yours), or picking their arm up at the wrist, using your hand, and moving it (this can become movement 'done to' the dancer). Normally, the first choice is a less imposing way of assisting, and also makes your experience of the movement more similar to the dancer's.

Creating a conducive environment

Safety, comfort, positive dancer/support worker relationships, and accessible communication all contribute towards a safe session where creativity through movement and dance can be explored. The number of stimuli within a room – visual, auditory and physical – may also need to be considered. At times it can be beneficial to cut down the stimuli within a session and isolate the experience that you are introducing and sharing with the dancers. *Restricting other stimuli isolates and so purifies and strengthens the learning experience.*

> **Example**
> ➤ Turn off or lower the lights.
> ➤ Lie or sit on mats (experiencing safe support via the floor but freedom from a wheelchair, see *Practical and logistical points to remember* on page 3).
> ➤ Play a sound on a quality instrument. Then stop playing and experience silence. You may repeat this several times: play – stop, play – stop, play – stop.
> ➤ Ask the dancer to make a movement (or to suggest a movement that you should make) that reflects the sound of that instrument. Then stop and be still. Repeat this several times.
> ➤ This exercise allows the dancer to explore and experience the contrast between movement and stillness.

It is crucial that sufficient time is allowed for participants to explore and experience movements

1

The last example also illustrates how a dance/movement concept can be compounded through sound (using musical instruments). This activity encourages participants to listen (rather than just to hear). It also builds a pattern of anticipation for the start and end of the sound and accompanying movement, known as *physical listening* (see the *Key skills* section in *Body talk* on page 22). The activity also creates a shared experience between participants.

Alternative ways of experiencing different movements

Pupils with limited movement must be given opportunities to experience a variety of movements, dynamics and patterns using alternative means. This enables them to experience movements that are not usually possible.

Example

Moving quickly, darting through space and creating swift changes of direction can be experienced through:

➤ dancers using their wheelchairs to enable them to travel at different speeds and in different directions, or

➤ a dancer lying on a piece of lycra and being dragged and swirled by staff across the floor. The dancer can indicate when and where changes of direction are to take place.

The experience of moving through the air (leaping) can be achieved by:

➤ assisted lifts, or

➤ a dancer lying in lycra and being carried or swung.

In addition, dancers can use their wheelchairs in different ways – tilting them sideways or forwards and using them as a focus for balance.

Dancers can use their wheelchairs to enable someone else to travel, or balance. In these instances the dancer using the wheelchair is the enabler.

A dancer who normally uses a wheelchair can use a standing frame to experience being vertical and working from a standing position (i.e. working at a different level).

Health and safety issues must be considered in relation to individual staff and dancers before attempting any of the above activities.

Dancers can use their wheelchairs to enable someone else to balance

Using different qualities of touch

By using different qualities of touch on a hand, face or foot, you can create small dances.

1

13

Example

When working with a partner:

➤ check that the recipient understands and is happy about being touched,

➤ check with physio/medical and/or teaching staff that this activity is acceptable in relation to the dancer's physical management programme, and

➤ identify a 'safe' body area to work on, e.g. hand, back, arm, that is non-threatening to the participant's personal privacy.

Experiment with different kinds of touch, using hands or props. Try:

➤ firm pressing,

➤ tapping finger tips,

➤ stroking,

➤ pushing – with the heel of the hand, knuckles, or thumbs.

Vary:

➤ the rhythm of touch,

➤ the patterns you are tracing, e.g. circling or straight lines,

➤ the speed of touch,

➤ the dynamic of touch, e.g. sustained, gentle, lively staccato,

➤ the spacing of touch on body surface, e.g. on outside of area, in centre,

➤ the direction of touch, e.g. upward strokes or zigzag lines.

Play music that relates to your 'touch dance' (or use music as the stimulus) to enhance the experience of the dynamics and qualities of your touch dance.

Cues from your partner (verbal and non-verbal) will indicate likes, dislikes, choices, etc. It is vital that you are acutely aware of these cues and react to them (see *Body talk* on page 19).

Cues from your partner will indicate likes, dislikes and choices

Props can vary the type and quality of touch. Use:

➤ clean paintbrushes in different thicknesses for brush strokes or stippling,

➤ straws to trace lines or blow through,

➤ feathers (be careful of tickling if it is unbearable to the dancer),

➤ fabric – scarves or ribbons of different textures, such as velvet, wool, hessian or silk,

➤ different types of brushes – soft bristles or a wire brush used very gently,

➤ natural objects, such as stones that are cool, smooth or uneven, or conkers,

➤ balls of different sizes and textures to roll, press gently or bounce across the surface of the body, e.g. beach balls, tennis balls or small rubber balls.

Be sure to get feedback from your partner and appraise as you would for a piece of dance (see *Tomorrow's dance makers* on page 65).

For example:

➤ Were there any touches that the dancer disliked?

➤ How did the 'touch dance' relate to the music?

➤ Did the dancer feel changes of speed?

➤ What patterns did the dancer enjoy?

➤ What differing dynamics and qualities of touch did the dancer experience?

➤ Did the 'touch dance' have a beginning, middle and end?

➤ What would the dancer like to have changed?

1

Basic choreographic skills such as:

➤ use of space,

➤ use of speed,

➤ changes in direction,

➤ use of rhythm, and

➤ varying dynamics

are all used in the last example. However, instead of bodies moving, the 'dances' are the different types of 'touch'.

Can your partner be the choreographer and direct (using verbal or non-verbal communication) a 'touch dance'?

Props or other art forms may maximise the movement and dance experience within a session. Musical instruments can be used in a variety of ways including:

➤ translating the sound an instrument makes into a movement – reflecting the dynamic and quality,

➤ playing an instrument with different body parts, e.g. playing an ocean drum with your foot then removing the drum and repeating the movements on the floor, in the air, or against other surfaces (including a partner's hands or back), moving the instrument from side to side to create a sound – exaggerating and minimising the movement and accompanying sound.

Another idea is to use light and shadows.

Creating shadows

Example

Using a screen and back-lighting, dancers who have minimal movement can create large moving shadows. This may help them to choreograph their movements.

Example

Whilst working with a group of children who normally use wheelchairs, and using the theme of mining (linked to their history curriculum), we created a dance that took place on the floor. We experimented with:

➤ rolling from our stomachs to our backs,

➤ balancing on our sides halfway between being on our fronts or our backs,

➤ turning and spinning on our stomachs and backs,

➤ sliding on our stomachs using our arms,

➤ travelling on our backs using our shoulders.

We also held torches with the beams shining on the ceiling and choreographed the beams to make different formations and movements. We used choreographic devices, such as canon and unison, as used in any dance composition.

1

15

These examples maximise the movement of the dancer and enable small movements to have a big impact. When watching someone with limited movement dance, it is common for people first to focus on what is *not* moving, before seeing a small, contained movement. *So it is vital to find opportunities to maximise the contribution of small movements.* It is also vital to instil the ethos that small movements are as valuable as larger ones within dance sessions.

It is also vital to instil the ethos that small movements are as valuable as larger ones within dance sessions

Choreographic devices

The use of *choreographic devices* to develop work is another choice and possibility open to you, as a leader. You may feel it is not relevant, however, particularly when dancers and support workers are initially getting used to moving together.

Using choreographic devices does not need to involve long complicated dances. Simple devices can develop dance material.

Options include:
➤ repeating movements and building sequences,
➤ varying dynamics,
➤ varying use of speed,
➤ varying use of levels,
➤ question and answer phrases – where one person makes a movement and the second person responds to that movement by making their own (this can develop as a movement conversation),
➤ mirroring,
➤ joining with other pairs to form small groups then moving, together and separately, in those groups.

Dancers can make choices such as:
➤ selecting their preferred movements,
➤ indicating when and where their partner moves,
➤ indicating the start of a phrase, e.g. they choose when to start.

Dancers can indicate
when and where their
partner moves

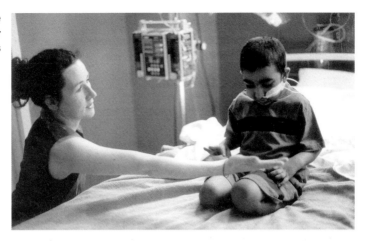

Example

Whilst working in a hospital ward with a 12-year-old girl who had to lie flat on her back, we first explored what movements were possible using arms and hands. Once she had selected the movements she liked, she directed her mother, grandmother and myself, and created a short dance piece in which she participated. Thus, she was both choreographer and dancer.

The piece centred around her bed, but to include elements such as changes of level she instructed us to perform some of the movements above her own hands, and others moving away, underneath and around her bed.

Physically, she was the least able person at that time. However, as well as being a participating dancer, she was the decision-maker. She controlled the piece, as well as dancing in it.

At a time in her life when she was totally dependant – virtually everything had to be done for her (washing, fetching, lifting, manoeuvring) – and treatment decisions were being made for her by medical staff, it was of great significance that she took control and made decisions within the dance session.

Varying the experience

A dance session can be boring and tiring for someone with very limited movement but a lively intellect, especially if they are working with more able-bodied dancers and are continually repeating the same small range of possible movements. It can also be potentially dangerous for dancers with particular conditions to over-exert and exercise the same group of muscles (as in the example above). It is important to be aware of this and to vary the dancer's role within the session by asking them to take turns as:

➤ appraiser,

➤ dance critic,

➤ rehearsal director,

➤ choreographer.

1

17

Some dancers may also need physical 'time out'. This time can be spent reflecting, verbally re-capping, considering choreographic choices or purely resting.

Caring for everybody's body

Consider everyone's health and safety within dance sessions. You need to ensure that:

➤ any lifting and use of hoists is carried out by qualified staff,

➤ staff are aware of their own bodies, e.g. back care (especially if a lot of cradling or rocking takes place),

➤ you are aware of any degenerative conditions,

➤ physical time out is built into sessions as and when appropriate (These can be taken on an individual basis, or as a whole group. Whilst taking physical time out people can still be involved by observing others' work.),

➤ you have an on-going awareness of individual dancers' physical management programmes,

➤ you have an on-going dialogue with teaching and care staff and physio/medical staff, to gain information and check out your ways of working.

SUMMARY POINTS

➤ *Think* how you will have to adapt your activities so that all the dancers with whom you are working can access a wide range of movement experiences.

➤ *Ensure* that support workers have a clear understanding of the implications and skills of being a facilitator rather than a leader.

➤ *Value* and recognise the significance of small movements.

➤ *Be constantly aware* of the need to see, sense and feel small movements and contributions, and include these within activities.

➤ *Keep* all levels of communication open – find points of access for all.

➤ *Aim for high quality work*, as always.

➤ *Safety – Comfort – Enjoyment.*

1

Body talk

Working in a non-verbal way

For those of us who live and communicate as part of a verbal world, working non-verbally can be a challenge! For verbal people, a lot of importance is placed upon the use of words in our learning, communicating and day-to-day life. The irony is that whilst verbal aspects of life are seen as the main way of interacting with other people, there are more forms of non-verbal communication (body language, facial expressions, etc.) taking place at any one time in our daily lives. Unfortunately, we are not encouraged to explore and value our capacity to express ourselves non-verbally, or to recognise other people's physical signs and movements. We are not well equipped by our education or daily experiences to interact confidently with others in a non-verbal way.

Why no words?
There are many reasons why someone is not able to, is partially able to, or chooses not to communicate verbally, including:
➤ learning difficulties,
➤ medical conditions (short or long term), e.g. some forms of cerebral palsy,
➤ trauma, such as a head injury or stroke resulting in loss of verbal language,
➤ age-related illnesses, such as dementia,
➤ psychological illnesses.

There are many reasons why someone is not able to, is partially able to, or chooses not to communicate verbally

2

19

Conditions such as those listed above may lead to:

➤ lost or under-developed speech,
➤ difficulty with speech (making it difficult for others to understand what individuals are saying),
➤ no speech,
➤ use of a communication aid.

There are two distinct groups of non-verbal participants:

1) Those who have difficulty with verbal language, but who do understand verbal communication. They may or may not have intellectual impairments.
2) Those who have severe and complex learning needs, e.g. severe intellectual impairments, no verbal language, and for whom verbal language is perplexing and not their preferred learning style.

For these two groups, there are two distinct ways of working with non-verbal participants:

1) Working verbally – knowing an individual's communication strategies is vital to enable a two-way process where participants express ideas and give feedback. However, sessions can be run as they would be for verbal students.
2) Working non-verbally – where minimal verbal or spoken language is used. These sessions will involve a lot of experimentation and improvisation, where the dancers are encouraged to respond openly and genuinely to each other.

Working non-verbally

Sessions will still have a basic format of:

➤ warm up,
➤ developing material,
➤ warm down/relaxation,
➤ conclusion.

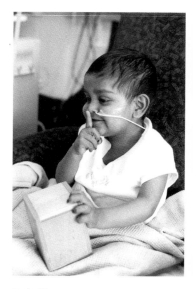

Verbal language may not be a dancer's preferred learning style

However, the vast majority of the dance work will be based on improvisation (see the *Relevant starting points* section later in this chapter for examples). Dancers will be required to work together (this can be with one staff worker per dancer or per small group of dancers). Use few or no rules and see what happens. For example, dance alongside each other – copy each other or take it in turns to lead the movements – and see what develops. Small dances will

2

emerge from people's own ideas, their movements and their reactions to each other, music or props.

Echoing, reflecting, connecting, picking up on responses, and moving into the unknown are all part of improvisation.

Why use non-verbal methods?

➤ Dance and movement may be a person's preferred learning style (see the *Co-motion* section on page 53).
➤ Working non-verbally enables you to focus fully on the physical experience of moving and dancing. This is a valuable experience for all – regardless of disabilities.
➤ Dance can be a pathway for making a connection with people in a way that is not possible in other aspects of their life.

Working non-verbally can offer:
➤ direct and spontaneous communication,
➤ opportunities to build relationships – in this context relationships mean contact and engagement between individuals and other dancers through dance,
➤ opportunities for dancers to work as equals,
➤ time to develop unique movement and dance material that emerges within the moment – you may not be able to re-capture this,
➤ a freedom to express oneself – particularly for those for whom verbal communication is a struggle,
➤ a kinaesthetic experience – one in which there is a pure focus on feeling the movement.

Introducing non-verbal work in dance sessions

When and how you introduce non-verbal methods will depend on the situation. Points to consider are:
➤ Staff training – this should take place before you start using non-verbal methods. It needs to clarify ways of working and the role of staff within sessions.
➤ Gradual introduction – if people have not worked non-verbally before, or dance sessions have been run differently, be sensitive in how you introduce change.

Working non-verbally can offer direct and spontaneous communication

2

21

When working non-verbally you will need:
Staff
➤ The correct number of staff for the ratio you need/wish to work with.
➤ Staff who can participate actively in the dance session.
➤ Staff who understand what their role is within the sessions and different ways of working (see *Small dances – big value* on page 7).

Key skills
➤ Physical listening – being able physically to feel initiation of, and changes in, movements, stillness and breathing rhythms as you are dancing with someone.
➤ Respectful physical contact – being respectful of other dancers' bodies, space and movement contributions throughout a dance.
➤ Awareness – being particularly vigilant as you only have non-verbal information from dancers who are not able to articulate verbally their experience, likes, dislikes and needs.
➤ Reacting to cues – being able to see, sense, hear and physically feel responses from the dancers.

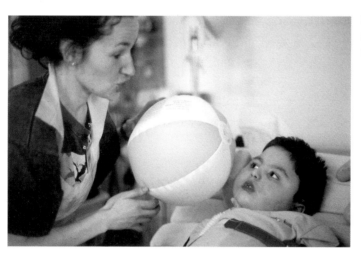

Respectful physical contact and reacting to non-verbal cues from a dancer

The essential element for working in a non-verbal way is that all participants, including staff, feel comfortable with improvisation.

What responses could you get?

Responses will include:

➤ showing like and dislike,
➤ indicating a choice, e.g. the direction to travel in,
➤ initiating new movements,
➤ changes of speed,
➤ changes of direction,
➤ changes of dynamics,
➤ need for a rest break,
➤ need for refreshment.

Relevant starting points

These are numerous, as for any dance session, and should be chosen in relation to specific learning objectives. Tried and tested possibilities include:

➤ Movements – mirroring, developing and improvising movements and creating short dances.
➤ Music – playing a particular piece of music or using instruments as a starting point for dancers to improvise to. Alternatively, dancers can explore how to move instruments and make sounds themselves.
➤ Props – introducing a prop or props and inviting dancers to experiment and improvise with them individually, in pairs or in small or large groups depending on the prop and learning objectives (See *A bag of tricks?* on page 81).
➤ Environment – the environment you dance in will provide new surroundings and stimuli to explore and react to. You can change your dance venue, e.g. dancing outside, in a different room or on a stage. You can also alter your constant venue by varying the space you use. Very contained and small spaces can be created using masking tape to make shapes and zones on the floor, with routes to and from each area. Different floor coverings can create different tactile environments to move over and around, including some that make noises, such as bubble wrap.

Making non-verbal interventions

When you can't ask for changes or identify areas for development verbally, you have to use non-verbal ways of intervening and encouraging change. The following have worked and can be used in both non-verbal and verbal sessions.

2

23

Changing combinations of partners or small groups

We all have our own preferred and familiar dynamics and movements. Working non-verbally enables us to experience someone else's way of moving – their types of movements, pace, use of space and dynamics. Improvising with other dancers enables us to develop new material that is outside our familiar range. The material is partly 'ours' and partly from our co-dancer/s – a unique combination.

Varying stimuli

Utilising a range of stimuli (music, light, props, sound) will help to:

➤ extend dancers' experience of stimuli,

➤ prompt different responses,

➤ enable a range of 'ways in' for dancers. For example, one individual may find tactile stimuli particularly inspiring, whilst another may enjoy responding to music or sounds.

Change the mood of the music

This can prompt a very instant change of dance and movements. Music from different cultural styles can evoke very different responses.

Introducing different movement dynamics

When improvising with someone, you (or they) can vary the type of movements you are doing. For example, large, powerful and expansive movements can be followed by gentle, articulate hand shapes or head movements.

Changing the environment

Using muted lighting or blocking off a space to make it smaller and more intimate may result in different types of movement and dances.

Outcomes of sessions

Non-verbal sessions can lead to different ways of showing work.

Performance

A process of repeating and developing material can be established in non-verbal sessions, so that 'pieces' can be created and performed.

2

24

Sharing work

Improvisation can lead to dances that cannot be recaptured. Sometimes the nature of the dancers may mean that a live performance is not the most positive way to show work. Instead, videoing and/or photographing work, or open workshops, may be more relevant (see the *Show and tell* section on page 71).

Challenges of working non-verbally

Working purely through dance and movement can encourage equality between dancers. This is an important factor, which can have mixed consequences.

Positive:

➤ Non-verbal dancers can feel empowered, able to participate on a par with peers, and to contribute actively within a session. This may not be the case in other lessons/scenarios.

Negative:

➤ Support workers may feel uncomfortable working alongside dancers on an equal footing. This change in the power balance may initially create unease for some staff. Staff training may be needed before the dance sessions begin.

➤ Dancers may initially feel uneasy and unfamiliar working on an equal basis with support workers who are normally 'in charge'.

Working purely through dance and movement can encourage equality between dancers

It is important to be aware of such reactions and encourage others to acknowledge them, without judging whether they are 'right' or 'wrong'. Learning to develop non-verbal relationships is a life-long process for us all. Anxieties can often disappear over a period of time as participants become more relaxed, more familiar with non-

2

25

verbal relationships, and engage with this way of working. Regular sessions over a long period are the ideal way to develop non-verbal work.

If anxieties increase and become obstructive, it may be that:
➤ the format of the session needs to be adapted (i.e. a longer warm up or ice-breaking section),
➤ particular individuals are not willing/able to be part of these sessions at present, and need to have the option of leaving the sessions,
➤ non-verbal work needs to be introduced slowly – into familiar and established dance sessions – before running whole sessions in that way.

Assessing non-verbal dance sessions

Each establishment will have its own assessment procedures, to which the following points may be added.

Be clear what *you are assessing*. Is it:
➤ a specific learning objective, e.g. the dancers' ability to create a duet,
➤ a dancer's engagement with dance, e.g. how the dancer is involved in the dance during the session – participating, watching and decision making,
➤ your leadership skills,
➤ the format of the sessions, e.g. was the warm up effective as a lead into the central theme/s?

Assessment can include feedback from:
➤ dancers – their reactions within sessions and before/after sessions,
➤ support workers involved in a session,
➤ education/care staff who know the student well, and can therefore be an invaluable reference point,
➤ your observations as session leader.

Feedback from dancers can come in many ways.

2

The following non-verbal factors can be significant clues to a dancer's experience of a non-verbal session:
➤ The level of a dancer's participation in a session – does this change

over time, indicating that the dancer is becoming more or less involved?

➤ A dancer's active contribution to a session – do they contribute movement ideas?

➤ A dancer's enjoyment of a session – are they enjoying specific parts of the session, and why? Do they show this through laughter, excitement and enthusiastic participation?

➤ Development of the range and types of movements used – does the dancer show an expanding awareness and understanding of dance?

➤ Whether the dancers are working together – is this happening in other lessons? What is the proximity between the dancers as they are dancing? Has this changed? For example, are dancers who initially worked in isolation now capable of relating and interacting with others? Or are dancers who always depend on others now able to feel secure when working alone?

➤ Whether a dancer is watching and showing awareness of others in the group.

➤ A dancer's use of space – has this changed? Are they working at different levels (high, medium, low), or moving through more space (not staying in 'their' corner/private zone)?

Example

When working with a group of non-verbal dancers with very challenging behaviour, over a period of time I noticed that all the dancers responded differently to the dance sessions, and these responses varied from week to week.

After a few weeks a member of staff reported that one specific dancer was whistling the tune of our warm-up music on the way to sessions. This was a dancer who seemed shut off during the session, barely participating, but who was increasingly watching others. His whistling indicated that he had related to the sessions in some way, and was certainly happy to come to them. His participation increased slowly over a period of months, until he eventually became a very active dancer within the group.

His whistling was a vital piece of feedback for me as the session leader, since it told me that he was connecting with the work and so gave me the security to encourage him strongly to dance.

In many cases it can take weeks or months to see a slight change. When leading a session there is so much to see and do that it may be helpful to have an 'informed observer' watching – someone who knows the dancers and can feed back on what they see.

When we are at a loss for words, our bodies are still speaking.

2

SUMMARY POINTS

➤ *Know* your non-verbal dancers – and select or create the appropriate way of working with them.

➤ *Ensure* that support workers are clear and comfortable with your ways of working.

➤ *Be aware* – you must be constantly vigilant and open to participant's non-verbal responses by listening, watching and feeling.

➤ *Intervention* – develop non-verbal ways of guiding the sessions.

Dancing on the ceiling

Working with high energy participants

'High energy behaviour' is an umbrella term used to describe a range of behaviours (see *Example* below). It is one type of 'challenging behaviour', which can span an enormous range of behaviours and related medical or psychological conditions. This chapter focuses on high energy and the challenges that this can present within a dance session. There are no easy answers, but there are ways of channelling high energy behaviour into high quality achievement.

Challenging behaviour of any kind can be exhausting, rewarding, relentless, exciting and can push you to your creative limits. Creative solutions and realistic aims are the key to turning a challenging situation into a creative and rewarding one.

Example

Whilst working on a Hospital School's Dance Project a few years ago, one of my groups of young dancers (seven boys, one girl, 10–12 years old) was particularly challenging. All the group members:

➤ had a lot of energy,
➤ had short attention spans,
➤ enjoyed fast, high impact activities,
➤ displayed disruptive behaviour at times,
➤ acted as a trigger for each other's behaviour, often 'winding each other up',
➤ enjoyed attempting feats that could be dangerous to themselves and others – trying big activities at full pelt with little regard for, or notion of safety, e.g. jumping from heights, falling, jumping and catching hold of, or throwing things.

I had previously run sessions with one or two such individuals within a larger group, but a whole group was a different challenge! The specific needs of the individuals and the speed of response required from me as a leader were demanding and at times felt relentless.

Causes of high energy behaviour

A range of factors can contribute to high energy behaviour, including:

➤ Medical factors – e.g. hyper behaviour related to uncontrolled diabetes, neurological damage or delay, a chemical imbalance within the body.

➤ Sociological/environmental factors – other people not providing an environment that helps the young person focus their behaviour, or an overly tight and constricting environment that a young person rebels against.

➤ Emotional and psychological factors.

Impact of high energy dancers

If their energy is not channelled, high energy dancers can possibly harm:

➤ the ethos of the group,

➤ themselves,

➤ other dancers,

➤ the physical environment – room, equipment, etc.

High energy dancers need:

➤ clear boundaries,

➤ consistency,

➤ relevant stimuli,

➤ relevant pace of session and change of stimulus/activity,

➤ physical movement that wears them out,

➤ attention from others,

➤ appropriate support.

Staffing

Ensure that you have a suitable support worker to dancer ratio in the dance session. You may need to run staff training prior to dance sessions, to clarify support workers' roles and the ways of working within a dance session. This training could include:

➤ support workers' sensitivity to the dance session and ways of working,

➤ support workers' knowledge of methods of working with dancers who, if challenged negatively, may exhibit unacceptable behaviours which escalate and lead to loss of control. Support workers need to be prepared to compromise, making positive outcomes wherever possible, rather than negative confrontations.

3

Picking up cues

In the dance session, look at what is happening and consider the dance and movement potential within the situation.

Warm ups may need to echo participants levels of energy and activity

> **Example**
> If students come into the session running, you could start the warm up with everyone moving at speed, and then develop this into other movement sequences, such as travelling at speed … turn/roll … freeze.

Framework for behaviour

It is important to set clear, defined boundaries. Defining behaviour boundaries leaves dancers with clear decisions.

> **Example**
> During a dance session, a group from a hospital school began banging on radiators. Recognising the dance potential, I informed them that just banging was not acceptable.
>
> If we were going to bang on radiators we needed a rhythm. Also, did we just have to use hands? What other body parts could we use?
>
> We then experimented with banging on other surfaces – floor, doors, etc. and then introduced stamps, claps, jumps, shuffles and so on, until we had a sequence of dance moves.

This type of activity could be introduced non-verbally, working alongside a dancer who is banging on a radiator. Provide an underlying beat or elaborate on their rhythm, using your fingernails, feet, elbows, etc. to make rhythms, and see how the dancer responds (see *Body talk* on page 19).

Using music

Music can greatly influence the mood of a dance session and the feelings and responses of all who hear it.

➤ Music with a fast manic beat and energy may evoke similar states in dancers. If you use such a piece of music, be very clear how you are going to channel energy and ensure that the activity remains safe for all involved.

➤ Changing between music styles can manipulate the speed and size of responses, and the mood of a dance session. Make sure you have a wide range of music and sounds to use.

3

Breaking the momentum of energy

In most dance sessions the leader plans to build and maintain a momentum of energy/activity throughout a session. However, when working with high energy dancers you may need to build in breaks and changes of pace to keep the energy under control.

You may need to build in breaks and changes of pace

Useful breaks include:

➤ *Relaxation times* – ask the dancers to listen and feel their heart beat, and to feel it slow down as they take deep breaths and enjoy a period of stillness.
Or, talk the dancers through a relaxation exercise (clenching and releasing various muscle groups, concentrating on different body parts, etc.) (See *Dance ideas* on page 95.)

➤ *Contemplation/reflection* – the dancers are still – sitting or lying – and you ask questions about the dance they have been doing, for them to consider. (See *Dance ideas* on page 95.)

➤ *Rest times* – getting refreshment.

➤ *Decision making* – ask participants to make a decision, e.g. What piece of music shall we use next? What shall we do next? Do you want to work in pairs or large groups? However, make sure that you can deal with the outcomes of the choices you offer.

➤ *Contrasting activity* – involve the dancers in a different, stand-alone activity, such as being rocked in lycra, or lying underneath a parachute. Although this activity involves only one individual at a time, often the anticipation of a reward (i.e. their turn) enables dancers to lie or sit still while they are waiting. Consider the health and safety issues of the activity (see *Practical and logistical points to remember* on page 3).

➤ *Cool downs* – contrast the dynamics of fast, high impact dance work by introducing challenging balances and stretches.

Introducing props

Different stimuli can catch interest and enable participants to explore something 'new' (see *A bag of tricks?* on page 81). But beware! Props can also become potential weapons. You must have clear strategies for channelling enthusiastic or challenging responses.

A dancer being rocked in lycra

Rocking in lycra

Lay a very large piece of good quality lycra flat on the floor. With a dancer lying in the middle of it, four adults take a corner each and

3

lift it gently, slowly taking the dancer's weight. The dancer now lies in the lycra like a hammock and can be:

➤ rocked to and fro,
➤ travelled around the space,
➤ raised and lowered.

For the dancer to be able to relax and absorb the experience of the activity, they must have trust in the adults holding the lycra.

➤ The participant must feel safe, so keep movements gentle.
➤ Ensure that the participant is lying safely and comfortably.
➤ Keep up a running commentary on what is happening and what is about to happen, to help the dancer feel safe.
➤ Agree at the beginning of the activity that you will stop should the dancer indicate.
➤ All those lifting the lycra need to be clear what their role is and what is expected.
➤ Consider the health and safety issues of the activity (see *Practical and logistical points to remember* on page 3).

Under a parachute/material

A dancer lies on the floor under a large piece of light material

The dancers lie on their backs or sides on the floor, while support workers or other dancers hold the edges of a large piece of light material/parachute above them. The support workers move the parachute material in a variety of ways, e.g. raising and lowering it, rippling, etc. The dancers may feel, hear and see the movements of the parachute.

➤ Ensure that the dancers under the parachute are not flicked or hit by the parachute, e.g. if it is lowered quickly.
➤ Those responsible for holding and manoeuvring the parachute need to know what is expected of them.
➤ A verbal commentary on what is happening and what is about to happen may help the dancers feel safe.
➤ Consider the health and safety issues of the activity (see *Practical and logistical points to remember* on page 3).

Positive risk taking

Taking risks can be exhilarating and fulfil a need or desire to be experimenting 'on the edge'. Directed well it can also instil in the dancers:

➤ self-confidence,
➤ physical self-awareness,

3

33

➤ team work,

➤ high quality work that is exciting to watch,

➤ motivation to explore other aspects of dance.

Managing a risk-taking activity well is the key to success for all involved.

➤ Ensure that you make a risk analysis of each individual's behaviour before embarking on the activity.

➤ It is crucial to provide vital and vibrant creative stimuli, such as a physical demonstration or video clips, plus a clear message of how the activity needs to be carried out.

➤ Pupils need to have a very clear understanding of what the task is and how to achieve it. For example, to jump over a partner while they are rolling towards you at high speed you need to wait X number of counts, take off here and land there.

➤ Plan the activity in slow motion – exactly how stunts, lifts, etc. are to be executed.

➤ Pupils need to understand that dangerous behaviour may result in injury and what the consequence of such behaviour will be, e.g the activity will stop.

The positive outcomes of the dance activity need to outweigh the 'satisfaction' a participant may get from negative actions. For example, the sensations of lifting each other, or throwing and catching objects at high speed as part of a dance, must be more exciting and rewarding than hitting someone, or throwing the objects to destroy them (or any other negative behaviour).

Non-verbal leadership

It is important for you as leader to establish your presence physically. Your body language will speak volumes.

A leader who is:

➤ dressed appropriately,

➤ actively engaged in the session,

➤ physically assisting, demonstrating and enabling dancers to succeed,

➤ enjoying moving and dancing alongside dancers,

will create a contagious enthusiasm and commitment within the session which will impact on the dancers' experience and impressions.

Managing a risk-taking activity well is the key to success for all

Your body language will speak volumes

3

You may need to be in close physical proximity to dancers during risk-taking activities. This will enable you to intervene if necessary, and also shows that you are monitoring the activity closely.

Verbal leadership

Verbal interaction and encouragement throughout sessions will show a leader's investment and commitment to dancers. (See *Feedback*, below.)

Target setting

Identifying realistic targets with and for individuals can help to create positive experiences of achievement for dancers. Encouraging dancers to identify their own targets is a way of encouraging individuals to plan and take control of their experience.

Suitable targets may include:
➤ to contribute ideas within a small group setting,
➤ to lead a warm up activity.

Feedback

We all rely on feedback. Positive but earned feedback (i.e. not saying anything/everything is wonderful), can encourage dancers to stay involved with a session. Look for opportunities to praise specific positive behaviour – however fleeting. Young people with high energy behaviour may be accustomed to being told off and removed from groups or lessons. Consequently they may feel that they have very little to offer.

Feedback can take many forms:
➤ verbal comments and encouragement by the leader,
➤ taking photographs or videos of the dancers involved in quality work,
➤ external 'visitor' (Governor/Head of Year/Head teacher/Artist) invited to see and comment on work in progress,
➤ audience feedback/applause if the work is performed formally.

Time out zones

These can be designated spaces within the hall/gym/studio where dancers can have 'time out' from the dance session.

Positive but earned feedback can encourage dancers to stay involved with a session

3

35

A time out zone may be used for a number of reasons, such as:

➤ providing a space for individual dancers to withdraw from the session to relax and calm down if they have overworked physically;

➤ providing space for individuals to withdraw if they are not coping with the sessions emotionally (escalating anxiety), and need to be out of the immediate activity;

➤ providing a space that acts as a half-way option, i.e. a dancer is removed from the immediate activity but can still be involved as an observer, rather than leaving the room and therefore leaving the session;

➤ enabling individuals to observe others working and give feedback, therefore validating the work of others. Such an activity can also focus the individual's energy;

➤ encouraging individuals to acknowledge their need for 'time out' and being able to take the decision themselves, i.e. self-nominating for time in the zone, enabling dancers to begin to manage their own behaviour;

➤ part of a discipline strategy. Time in the zone may be the equivalent of a 'yellow card' being shown to a player in football – a warning but also a chance to re-enter and remain an active participant within the session, if their behaviour is appropriate.

Support workers and dancers need to have a common understanding of the use of this space.

There needs to be a clear strategy for using the zone, which considers:

➤ restricting the number of times a student can access the zone during a session,

➤ restricting the amount of time spent in the zone, e.g. 10 minutes maximum,

➤ who decides when a dancer needs time in the zone. Do students self-nominate themselves and opt to have time in the zone? Or does the leader or support worker direct students into the zone? If so, do students have the right to decline?

➤ whether the use of a time out zone is part of a discipline and control strategy. If the use of the time out zone is having little effect on disruptive behaviour, is the next step removing the dancer from the room and therefore the session? Is that clearly understood by dancers and support workers?

Used positively, a time out zone can encourage individuals to step back and take time to look, think and consider. For many young people with high energy, the skill of 'taking time out' to plan, organise thoughts and ideas or reflect does not come naturally. Encouraging dancers to do this enables them to develop skills that are transferable to all areas of life.

Discipline strategy

Each institution will have a behavioural/discipline policy. These strategies are designed to assist teachers and leaders and should also apply to visitors to the institution (visiting artists or teachers). Hence, you should expect appropriate behaviour (however that is defined by the institution) from dancers within your sessions.

A behaviour/discipline strategy can help to create consistency of expectation and procedure throughout an institution. Some pupils may be on specific behaviour management programmes with which you will need to familiarise yourself.

However, if you have a problem with part of such a procedure, e.g. approaches that jar with your ways of working, you need to address this situation.

1) Initially find out from support workers within your sessions why specific procedures are used and what the desired outcomes are.
2) Then explain how and why these are preventing you from working in the way you wish, e.g. not allowing experimentation.
3) Negotiate ways of working that are specific to the dance session. Keep your 'bottom line' clear.
4) Ensure that whatever is agreed is sanctioned by relevant senior staff if needed.

Giving dancers alternative roles

Some dancers may benefit from taking on different roles during the dance session. This is often useful for a dancer who cannot maintain concentration to develop an ongoing piece of dance, although their peers in the group can.

Roles can include:
➤ initially starting the dance piece by turning music on,
➤ performing as a dancer for a short section,

Some pupils may be on specific behaviour management programmes with which you will need to familiarise yourself

3

➤ collecting and delivering props or controlling slide projector/lights alongside a member of staff,

➤ performing as a musician – playing a percussion instrument and accompanying the dance piece.

In this way the dancer is constantly involved with the piece but in different ways. This enables them to stay as part of a group project but also provides variety.

Balance of physical and discussion time

Physical 'doing' activities are usually the most engaging for dancers with high energy. Lengthy debate and long discussions are not a productive experience for those who prefer to learn by physically exploring and doing. However, managing a relevant mix of doing and debating is important. You will need to:

➤ monitor dancers' engagement with the two different types of activities – doing and talking,

➤ use a variety of stimuli to introduce or illustrate a specific point in discussion, e.g. video clip, or a physical object (such as a ball bouncing to illustrate the physicality of jumping and landing).

Awareness of working relationships

Some dancers may engage fully in activities when directed in a large group, but flounder when asked to work with a partner or in a small group. This may be due in part to underdeveloped social skills that make negotiating, listening, exchanging and selecting ideas very challenging.

You may need to:

➤ utilise support workers to support and enable co-operative work in smaller groups, e.g. one member of staff to each group, whose role is to enable the process of 'working together'.

➤ use individuals' ideas but you, as leader, give them to the whole group to try out, rather than finding initial ideas in small groups. For example, ask: Has anyone got an idea of how we can move from here to there? Take an individual's suggestions and then get the whole group to try it all together.

➤ be aware of inter-personal dynamics within a group. For work in small groups, organise combinations of students that are most likely to work and therefore achieve.

Some dancers may benefit from taking on different roles during the dance session

3

38

Also be aware that dancers may flounder when working solo and may need the security of a clear teacher-led structure.

Using a variety of approaches

Dancers with short concentration spans can tire quickly of a particular activity, so it is important to have a number of different ways of exploring your chosen theme or idea. Approaches include:

Use a variety of approaches when exploring your theme to keep the interest of dancers with short concentration spans

➤ physically exploring,
➤ watching video clips,
➤ drawing ideas, e.g. body shapes,
➤ videoing dancers and watching it together – identifying good work and specific areas for development. Remember to obtain permission to video the dancers (see *Practical and logistical points to remember* on page 3).

Resources

You will need a range of resources to maintain the dancers' interest and as a basis for creative ways of introducing and exploring dance ideas.

Resources that will be useful include:

➤ music,
➤ sounds,
➤ musical instruments,
➤ physical props (see *A bag of tricks?* on page 81),
➤ photographs,
➤ videos,
➤ books – dance photographs can be very effective,
➤ slide projector,
➤ camera/video camera – to take photographs/video of sessions. Remember to obtain permission to photograph or video the dancers (see *Practical and logistical points to remember* on page 3).

Be aware that positive role models are very important. Choose your video clips, photographs, etc. with care.

Resources such as photographs, slides or video can be used as part of a final presentation, combining live performance with material from previous sessions, captured on film.

3

> **Example**
>
> For a dance piece based on 'clear body shapes and moving through the air', slides of dancers leaping and jumping through the air in clear exciting positions could be projected on to a plain back wall, or sheet of plain fabric on the wall. In this way, positive, high quality images of work from previous sessions, combined with a live dance performance, creates a strong positive impact and presence for the dancers.

Showing work

There are many ways of presenting work (see *Show and tell* on page 71).

Dancers with high energy can be desperate to perform

At times, dancers with high energy can be desperate to perform but:

➤ they may not be able or prepared to sustain and develop work to a performance level,

➤ their unpredictable behaviour may pose a threat to their own and others' health and safety.

Live performance

If you are opting to create a live performance with dancers with high energy, you will need to consider:

➤ utilising support workers – use staff who have been involved throughout the sessions and are aware of their role within a performance as well as their role of supporting the dancers and managing their behaviour;

➤ dance material – use dance material that the dancers enjoy and that they can perform successfully;

➤ length of performance – ensure that the length of concentration required is realistic and achievable for the dancers;

➤ accompaniment – choose music/sound that the dancers enjoy;

➤ costumes – dancers must be comfortable and feel good in what they are wearing. Consider whether particular costumes or accessories may help dancers to feel comfortable when performing, e.g. masks, face painting. Costumes can enhance the sense of event and kudos for the dancers;

➤ audience – choose your audience with care. First-time performers particularly will need a receptive audience;

➤ combining other elements – remember that you can use slides, video, etc. along with live performance. Remember to obtain permission to photograph or video the dancers (see *Practical and logistical points to remember* on page 3).

Involving everyone in the session

If a group includes a small number of dancers with high energy, you will need to consider how you can involve everyone in ways that enable them to achieve and contribute positively.

You will need to:
➤ know the needs of individuals and their preferred learning styles;
➤ ensure that you offer a range of tasks or ways of working;
➤ give all the dancers a chance to try different ways of working (e.g. drawing dance ideas, brainstorming words for movement ideas), so that such activities are not seen as punishment or as less valid contributions;
➤ validate all ways of working within sessions (e.g. drawing dance ideas is as valid as writing words);
➤ ensure that everyone is contributing to an overall whole;
➤ ensure that support staff are clear of their role within differentiated tasks.

Overall, the most valuable sessions are those that are structured and where the ways of working guide dancers to manage and direct their own high energy and behaviour.

Creating situations where dancers can achieve is vital to developing confident and creative dancers.

3

41

SUMMARY POINTS

➤ *Create* activities that interest and engage dancers.

➤ *Develop* ways of working that enable dancers to achieve. Consider their preferred learning styles.

➤ *Support workers* need to be clear of what their role is and of the methods of working with dancers within the sessions.

➤ *Look* for the dance potential in every situation and every individual.

➤ *Flexibility* – respond to events as they arise and find ways to channel energy.

➤ *Be prepared!* Develop a varied bank of dance resources and ideas to draw from.

➤ *Aim* for high quality work.

With and without wheels

Dancers and wheelchairs – the creative possibilities

There are different reasons for people using a wheelchair. Avoid making snap judgements and decisions about *why* someone is using a wheelchair, how long they are likely to be using a wheelchair, *how they feel* about using a wheelchair, and *whether* they have an option of coming out of the wheelchair for periods of time.

A wheelchair is usually individually tailored to the person who uses it, so swapping chairs is not recommended practice. Using 'spare' wheelchairs, with the agreement of physio/medical staff within the school/institution you are working in, will enable other dancers to experience work in wheelchairs.

There are infinite creative ways of generating exciting, strong and articulate dance material where the wheelchair becomes an extension of the dancer in it, or another dancer within the dance.

Types of wheelchair

There are basically two types of wheelchair – electric and manual.

Electric wheelchairs are battery operated and can be very heavy. Most of them can also be operated manually. They enable someone with a limited range of movement and/or strength to have independence of movement in a chair.

Generating creative dance material

4

43

Manual wheelchairs are quite heavy, sturdy structures, and are used by a range of people:

➤ Someone using a manual chair may be reasonably strong and able in their upper body and able to push the wheels and manoeuvre themselves around in the chair.

➤ Someone awaiting an electric chair may use a manual chair. They may not have sufficient strength to manoeuvre themselves and so may have a carer to push the wheelchair.

➤ Someone who does not have the intellectual capabilities to operate an electric wheelchair may use a manual wheelchair with a carer to push it.

In or out of the wheelchair

When deciding whether a dancer should come out of a wheelchair for a dance session, the main issue to consider is: *"For this dancer, will coming out of the wheelchair be an enhancement to movement development?"* The decision should be made after discussion with the dancer, physio/medical and teaching/caring staff, all within the context of your dance session.

For this dancer, will coming out of the wheelchair be an enhancement to movement development?

It is a mistake to assume that coming out of a wheelchair automatically brings feelings of freedom and power for every individual.

Example

For an adolescent with a degenerative condition and full awareness of it (i.e. no intellectual impairment), an electric wheelchair may mean independence and power, which they may not wish to relinquish. For this individual, working on the floor unsupported could lead to feelings of being further disabled.

However, in some cases the opportunity to work safely out of a wheelchair can be enormously beneficial, giving:

➤ freedom to move limbs and body in a different way, working on the floor supported by another person or mats, cushions, etc,

➤ an opportunity to work and move independently,

➤ an opportunity to work at a different level, e.g. on the floor, or standing in frame,

➤ an opportunity to utilise stronger parts of the body and achieve movements such as rolling, sliding, balancing on different body surfaces, etc. which are impossible in a wheelchair,

➤ an opportunity to work on the same level as others

It is a mistake to assume that coming out of a wheelchair automatically brings feelings of freedom and power for every individual

4

44

Other issues to consider

Level of support

The wheelchair gives the user a level of support. Can that safely be replaced by either human support (1:1 support) or physical support using bean bags, mats, cushions, etc?

Lifting out of the chair

The method of lifting needs to be age appropriate. For some dancers, their age, weight or size may mean that a physical lift contravenes all health and safety regulations, and also compromises their dignity and increases their feeling of dependency.

If a hoist is needed to lift someone from a chair, check that one is available and that staff are trained to operate it.

Staffing

Is staffing adequate and appropriate to manage manoeuvres both in and out of wheelchairs, and to provide the level of support needed for safe work throughout a session? Consider the health and safety issues for staff working in this way (see *Practical and logistical points to remember* on page 3).

Individual physical management programmes

Make sure you are aware of the physical management programmes for each dancer. For some dancers, being lifted out of their wheelchair may be totally inappropriate or non-viable. For example:

➤ a dancer on a 24-hour oxygen supply, which is attached to the chair;
➤ a dancer who has recently undergone an operation and is in a 'post operative stage' of recovery. This is particularly relevant when working on a hospital ward. Discussion with the patient, physio/ medical staff, and close family is an important part of understanding what action is relevant and desirable for that individual;
➤ a student who has brittle bones.

Caution
Whether or not a dancer can safely come out of a wheelchair may not be apparent when you first meet the individual. You need to collate all the information from the dancer, physio/ medical and teaching/care staff before you can collectively reach a decision.

4

45

Learning intentions

Being clear about the learning intentions in any session can help you to see whether dancers coming out of their wheelchairs would be either relevant or appropriate.

> **Example**
> In a session, the learning intention is to explore 'shape' in a variety of ways. As long as it is safe for students to come out of their wheelchairs and work on the floor, and they are happy to do so, working out of their wheelchairs would be both relevant and appropriate.

Other learning intentions for sessions where it may be relevant for dancers to leave their wheelchairs include:
➤ exploring locomotion,
➤ exploring working on and against a variety of surfaces,
➤ developing partner work based on the floor and/or that involves leaning, lying and taking weight,
➤ exploring the use of speed and dynamics.

All of these examples are relevant to any dancers and would give all dancers the option of working at floor level during a session.

Positioning the dancers

Having some people seated in wheelchairs and the remainder standing or lying supported on the floor can immediately create segregation. This is particularly true for groups who are meeting for the first time and have yet to explore the creative joys of difference and variety.

Also, working on the floor can be quite an 'intimate' way of working, which may be too challenging for a first session with a new group.

To avoid these difficulties:
➤ allow time for all dancers to work seated (on chairs), and on the floor, not using their legs, but concentrating on the upper body, head and arms.
➤ encourage dancers to work at different levels throughout the session. Make sure you are aware of the 'management' needed within a session to facilitate these changes and how much time it may take.
➤ vary the sitting/standing/lying combinations to introduce new

4

experiences for all the dancers in the session. Having everyone seated throughout every session is not necessarily a productive way for everyone to realise their full physical and creative potential. For example at different points in the session you could have:

➤ everyone seated at the same level
➤ some dancers in wheelchairs, others seated and some standing or sitting on the floor.
➤ everyone working on the floor.
➤ all the dancers working on specific body parts that are accessible to all.
➤ Make sure these variations change during the session.
➤ In a mixed group, ensure that dancers with disabilities do not always work seated in chairs or on the floor, while others work at a standing level (see *Co-motion* on page 53). Such a situation could make dancers feel disabled and different.

Setting tasks

As leader you should consider and evaluate the experiences that dancers are having within your session, in terms of learning about dance, working with others, working creatively and independently, etc. When dancers' experience of a session is also influenced by their mobility and understanding, it is crucial, though more difficult, to monitor their experience constantly, adapting and changing the session to enhance the quality of their experience.

When setting tasks, you need to be aware of the language you use (see *Co-motion* on page 53). You also need to be ready to adapt and translate movements so they are accessible to all dancers in the session.

Dancers working at a variety of levels, e.g. floor, seated, standing

---

Example

If you ask each member of the group to contribute a movement idea and someone makes a leg movement, unless everyone in the group can move their legs you will need to translate this movement to a different body part, such as arms. You can then give the whole group the option of doing the movement with

➤ legs,
➤ arms,
➤ arms and legs together.

As well as ensuring that everyone can participate, this also illustrates how a movement can be translated to different body parts to create choreographic variety.

4

To ensure that every dancer can access every task:

➤ set boundaries, such as focusing on specific areas of the body that all the dancers can move, so everyone starts from the same baseline,

➤ translate and adapt movements, e.g. to other body parts and in terms of size of movement, direction and speed.

The wheelchair and the dancer

There are many ways in which dancers can relate to wheelchairs, and they fall into two main categories:

Unison – moving in the same way as the chair

Dancer and wheelchair can move together:

➤ in the same direction,

➤ using the same dynamic, e.g. slowly, staccato,

➤ both still – a stationary chair and a still dancer within it,

➤ both moving – a moving chair and a moving dancer within it.

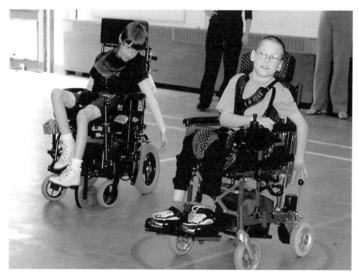

Dancer and wheelchair can move together

Unison can also include additional movements that complement the direction or dynamics of the movement. For example echoing the direction or speed of the chair using body shape (leaning in the direction that the chair is moving), or arm gesture (arm reaching, pulling, pointing). Other dancers in the group can echo the wheelchair's movements using gestures, etc.

Contrasting movements to the chair

Dancer and wheelchair can move in a contrasting manner:

4

Dancer and wheelchair can move in a contrasting manner

➤ where the chair is still (brakes on), the dancer can move in, on and around the chair (depending on the dancer's strength and mobility);

➤ the dancer can juxtapose the movement of the chair with contrasting dance movements. For example, if the chair is moving slowly, the dancer is performing fast, sharp movements.

The wheelchair as a piece of apparatus

A wheelchair can be used as a surface to balance, climb or lean on, pull or push against and pivot on, among many other things. This can lead to shapes and movements that are unique to a wheelchair and a body – they could not be reproduced without the wheelchair. If you are setting tasks that involve this sort of work, consider the following points.

➤ Choice – does the dancer wish to use the wheelchair in this way?

➤ Check before any balances or weight-taking that the points of support are safe for the dancer and the wheelchair. For example, with an electric wheelchair, check that the dancer is not leaning on the battery.

➤ Check that the dancer in the wheelchair (assuming there is one rather than an empty chair being used) is not being leant on, and is heavy enough to counter balance any pulling against the chair.

➤ Is the dancer in the wheelchair restricted by other dancers using the wheelchair as a creative focus and surface to work from?

➤ Does the chair become more important than the dancer within it?

Roles for dancers who use wheelchairs

It is imperative that you consider any dancers who use wheelchairs as dancers. Just like any other dancer, they can take different roles in the session:

➤ leader and instigator within dance sessions and pieces,

➤ creator of dance pieces,

➤ explorer – experimenting with creative tasks, e.g. notions of use of space, direction, shape, dynamics, etc.

➤ performer – as soloist, in duets or whole group pieces.

4

Dancers with limited movement who use wheelchairs

Some dancers do not use their wheelchairs independently, and have a carer/assistant to help them with their mobility by pushing the wheelchair. In this scenario, as leader you need to:

Explore how much the dancer can do for him/herself in terms of:
➤ range of physical movement,
➤ mode of communication – verbal, physical, communication aid or board,
➤ level of decision making,
➤ ability to recognise and make choices.

Define the role of the carer/assistant (see *Small dances – big value* on page 7), as:
➤ a support worker, co-dancer or enabler,
➤ an interpreter – picking up the dancer's non-verbal physical, visual and verbal cues.

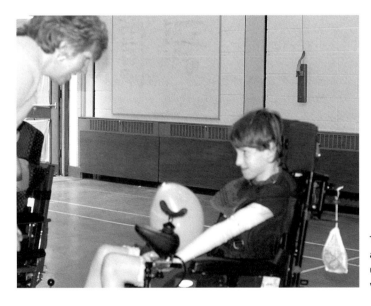

The role of assistant as interpreter, picking up the dancer's non-verbal cues

New ways of working may need to be developed for the assistant and the dancer in dance sessions. The physical positioning of the assistant in relation to dancer will be important, to maintain communication.

4

> **Example**
> Eye contact may be very important, so the assistant may need to work in front of, and in sight of the dancer. Therefore pushing the chair from behind for long periods may not be possible.

If a dancer has very limited movement, it is important to consider their experience of the session, and the possible variety of roles they can take, such as, choreographer or rehearsal director (see *Small dances – big value* on page 7).

SUMMARY POINTS

➤ *Know* your dancers and their wheelchairs (types of chair, workings, space required, etc).

➤ *Be aware* of individual dancers' physical management programmes and the implications for dancers working in or out of their wheelchairs. Also, be aware of dancers' emotional needs.

➤ *Explore and enjoy* the extra creative possibilities that a dancer who uses a wheelchair offers.

➤ *Remember* that the individuals who use wheelchairs are dancers and potential choreographers.

➤ *Support workers* – ensure that supporting staff have a clear understanding of their role within dance sessions.

➤ *Access* – ensure that all activities are accessible to all the dancers in the session.

➤ *Aim* for high quality work.

4

Co-motion

Inclusive dance sessions

An inclusive dance session is one that enables individuals with varying needs and abilities to have equal access to participating throughout. There are many aspects to consider in planning and delivering inclusive dance sessions: practical, logistical, artistic and creative.

Also, you need to take into account the diversity of needs within the group. *Disability* and *special needs* are very wide umbrella terms that cover extremely varied behaviours, physical abilities and learning processes/needs. It is important to be very clear about exactly what range of needs can be well met within your session. You need to be honest – and to consider whether your teaching/facilitation can inspire high quality work from all participants, equally.

The well-used phrase 'everyone is different' is true for us all, in terms of physical, emotional and creative make-up. We must erase the notion of 'the perfect body = the perfect dancer'. Then we have a rich starting point for any creative initiative, and its potential hinges on the importance of the dance leader and all participants being open to diversity.

Co-motion

Remember – an inclusive group of people provides such a wealth and variety of ways of moving, dancing, opinions, ideas, viewpoints and responses.

5

Top priorities

The top priority in planning an integrated session has to be *maintaining a high quality of experience for all participants*. Dancers within a session should be stretched, challenged and inspired and be able to develop a greater and deeper level of work in creative, artistic and physical ways.

When you balance this priority against the range of individual needs, and the practical support available, you will be well placed to make an honest assessment of how varied individual needs can be within one session.

The top priority in planning an integrated session has to be maintaining a high quality of experience for all participants

Initial questions to consider

➤ How diverse can the needs of dancers in the group be, if each individual is to be stretched to their physical and artistic potential?

Example

Can *you* facilitate a session where:
➤ dancers with gross motor impairments and complex learning needs can work successfully beside peers who have substantial previous dance experience?
➤ grandparents are working with high energy under fives?

➤ Is there adequate and appropriate staffing support?
➤ Are support workers clear about their role within the session? (See the *Preparation* section, later in this chapter.)
➤ Do you have strategies that will encourage differentiation and enable everyone to reach their current dance/movement potential?

Practical and logistical questions

➤ Are interpreters available if needed?
➤ Is there full wheelchair access to the dance space? Ensure that there is adequate room for dancers with wheelchairs to move freely.
➤ Are there toilets that enable wheelchair access? Check bathroom facilities and other access needs.
➤ Are there stairs that will be difficult or impossible for dancers with mobility issues?
➤ Is a wooden floor needed? (The vibrations of music and movements through a wooden floor may be particularly helpful to dancers who are deaf or have hearing loss).
➤ Is the floor level? Uneven flooring may be difficult for people

with mobility issues, e.g. someone walking with a walking frame.

➤ Are you well aware of the specific needs of those within your group?

Preparation

Good preparation lays a sound base for inclusive dance sessions.

Leader

Make sure you know as much as possible about the groups you are working with. Then your planning can be focussed on including everyone within your session.

Dancers working together in an inclusive session

Dancers

For many dancers from mainstream schools, an inclusive dance session may be their first experience of working with people with disabilities. For dancers from a special school, this may be their first experience of working alongside peers from a mainstream school. Separate introductory sessions may be needed to ensure that all participants are clear about what will be involved.

Good preparation lays a sound base for inclusive dance sessions

These separate sessions must have:

➤ clear intentions,

➤ activities, dance material and ways of working that are an indicator and a reflection of future work.

Example

When devising an inclusive choreographic project involving students with complex learning needs and a mainstream local first school, I scheduled a small number of initial sessions with each group separately to:

➤ enable each group to get used to me as a leader and my ways of working;

➤ enable me to get to know each group and any specific needs and issues that I needed to be familiar with, e.g. specific communication needs, preferred learning styles, how dancers worked together within their usual 'class' setting;

➤ allow time for participants to get used to dancing and moving together in ways that would be developed further in future sessions;

➤ allow time to explain:

  ➤ what would be happening in joint sessions (format),

  ➤ what the project was working towards (performance);

➤ allow time for discussion around:

  ➤ what they were expecting,

  ➤ how they felt and any anxieties,

  ➤ how we feel in new situations,

  ➤ what mainstream pupils understood by *special needs,*

  ➤ how different people react to different situations,

  ➤ how people learn in different ways.

5

55

Staff

Staff involved in the session need to be extremely clear about their role, including:

➤ what is required of them physically,

➤ suitable clothing to wear for dance work,

➤ ways of working – working alongside students, not taking over.

Learning styles

Everyone has their own particular learning style. Dancers who have complex learning needs may have very specific preferred styles of learning.

Example
Choreographic tasks that involve verbal instructions can be too perplexing for a dancer for whom verbal instructions are not his/her preferred learning style.

This does not mean that such students cannot be part of and contribute to a dance session, but *you need to ensure that the routes you are providing are relevant to them*. This could mean giving access through visual and physical means.

The wider the range of specific individual needs within the session, the more conscious you need to be about the structure, content and mode of communication you are using, and their relevance to all participants. (See *Body talk* on page 19.)

Communication

Whilst dance and movement is a way of communicating in its own right, it is important to ensure that *your* communication is relevant to all the dancers.

➤ Are communication boards, interpreters or signing needed? Ensure that this has been planned into your session.

➤ If you are working with an interpreter, be aware of where you are standing and where the interpreter needs or prefers to be in relation to you.

➤ If someone is lip reading, ask where he/she would like you to be in relation to windows, etc.

> **Example**
> Standing with your back to a window is not helpful for lip readers, as your mouth is then in shadow, or if it is a sunny day the person is looking directly into bright light.

Terminology

Be aware of the words and terms you are using. Familiar dance and movement phrases, that roll off the tongue easily in mainstream settings, can often use terminology that is exclusive and assumes that the dancers are able-bodied.

> **Example**
> Walk around the room for eight counts … walk on the beat … take eight steps …
> The instructions assume everyone can walk and only asks for this one form of movement.

Instructions similar to those above are very limiting. A more open instruction is accessible to all and does not limit responses.

> **Example**
> Move across the room for eight counts.
> The response can include many differing ways of travelling – rolling, wheeling, tummy sliding, etc.

Be aware of what you are asking of the group, what they ask from each other and whether the language used assumes an able-bodied response. Develop vocabulary that is relevant to everyone within your groups.

Using vocabulary that does not limit responses leads to far more creative work within any situation, whether or not the dancers in the group are able bodied.

The tone of dance sessions

True inclusion means that people's ideas, opinions and wishes are taken into account and that participants can be part of the decision making, and work in a collaborative way throughout a session. In order to be able to contribute their ideas and opinions, dancers will need to feel safe and confident in the dance session.

You will need to instil a group ethos that ensures:
➤ time for discussion, and a realistic time given for responses;
➤ people are listened to and seen, and their contributions are valued;

Be aware of the words and terms you are using

5

57

- the dance starts from what everyone *can* do, and what *is possible*;
- physical contact is respectful;
- different ways for participants to be a part of the choreographic and decision making process (see *Tomorrow's dance makers* on page 65) are considered;
- experimentation, involving ideas and moves that do not work so well, is valid too (choreography is about trying new ideas and movements);
- dancers are aware that some ways of working, movements, etc. may have to be adapted so that they are accessible for the whole group.

Time out

For some groups or individuals it may be relevant to build in 'time outs'. This may be to accommodate people's low energy levels, to increase people's sugar levels by having a drink, to de-escalate behaviour, for toileting reasons, or to allow natural discussion and working out of movements, etc.

Time outs can be introduced as:
- breaks where the session stops for a short time,
- relaxation moments within sessions, allowing people to absorb movements, thoughts and processes that have taken place,
- an opportunity for an individual to take time out within a session to be still, take stock and then re-enter the activity. Some leaders negotiate rules (maximum time allowed) and even mark out 'time out' spaces within the hall or studio they are working in.

Maintaining a balance

It is important to maintain a balance between the groups involved. No one group should dominate sessions in anyway, including:
- input of ideas,
- physical presence,
- decision making.

Ensure that one group is not used as a platform for the other, and do not allow one group to 'outshine' another.

Physical spacing

Initial spacing

When two groups work together for the first time they will probably naturally gather with the people they know, creating two separate groups. Initial activities that require participants to mix and move around the space can remedy this (see *Dance ideas* on page 95).

Be aware that some dancers need a lot of personal space and may become distressed if this is invaded quickly and without warning. If you are aware of dancers' needs prior to your sessions you can plan different activities, or ways of enabling that dancer to remain at a comfortable distance but still be involved.

Working on different levels

If some of the group normally use wheelchairs it is vital that they are not consistently the only ones working at a seated level, and therefore 'different'.

Participants working at different levels, e.g. seated on chair, on floor

To ensure movement is on different levels:
➤ have a number of chairs so there are always others seated,
➤ all dancers should work at a seated level at some point,
➤ all participants can work from the 'high' level of the wheelchair downwards.

There may also be others in the group who prefer to work on the floor. Again, incorporate the experience of floor work into the session for all participants. (See *With and without wheels* on page 43.)

The leader's use of space

Be aware of how you demonstrate ideas and material:
➤ Are you always standing?
➤ Do you work at a seated level?
➤ Do you use a variety of body parts? Remember some participants may not be able to use all body parts, so opportunities must be given to use mobile limbs.

When using a participant to demonstrate:
➤ Do you vary whom you choose? Giving a range of possibilities, using participants with different abilities, is important.
➤ Do you explain clearly what dance skill is being achieved?

5

59

Working together

As sessions develop, so will the confidence of all those involved. This means that tasks can require dancers to work together in an increasingly involved way. As with any dance session, varying combinations and size of groups will lead to different experiences. Try working with:

➤ partners,
➤ small groups,
➤ larger groups,
➤ as one group.

Creative tasks

These can have many starting points (see *Dance ideas* on page 95). If you use words to create dance phrases be aware of the types of words you are using (see the *Terminology* section, earlier in this chapter and *Movement words* on page 120).

Example

suspend   curl   reach   shift   turn
These instructions are open-ended. They can be applied to different body parts, so they enable accessibility.

walk   run   jump   tiptoe   leap
These words all assume use of legs and feet. They are not accessible to all.

Either do not use them *or* explore the notion of other body parts taking on that movement action. For example, the essence of a jump is the flight through the air. Can this be translated to a gesture of the arm, or of the torso and head?

New partnerships can be made through improvisation

Improvisation

This can be one of the purest ways of generating dance material. Asking dancers to work together with few or no rules allows them to explore movement and dance. New material can be developed, new challenges arise and new partnerships are made. Improvisation is not a chance to show off learned dance material or dance technique or tricks, but time to venture into the unknown and dance steps and movements that occur spontaneously.

The choreographic process

There are many ways of constructing dance pieces. Many choreographic tasks are relevant to inclusive dance sessions, as long

5

as they are accessible to all. However, a participant with disabilities can have ways of working and moving that introduce new creative ways of dancing and making dances.

Example

Working in a group that includes dancers with visual impairment may prompt the group to learn different skills, dancing together with touch and sound as a main common thread for all dancers. Cues and transitions are made via sound and music, or touch.

The way of moving together, responses to choreographic tasks, the communication between dancers and the dynamics arising from a particular mix of people will be unique in look, style and experience.

One person's concept of dance, their ways of working and particular needs can become a series of sessions that create a common and creatively richer way of working for all, rather than a 'problem solving' exercise in making adaptations to enable access.

Example

A piece exploring travelling will have far wider possibilities if wheels, feet and bodies moving across space are involved. As long as the choreographic tasks do not limit people to standing, walking and running, and therefore exclude people using wheelchairs, etc. a more diverse piece may emerge.

Reviewing the sessions

It is vital to review constantly how inclusive sessions are, and whether new strategies need to be introduced as a group develops. Honesty when reviewing your sessions is the best way to ensure that

5

participants have a quality dance experience.

Be on the look out at all times for dancers who may be feeling uncomfortable. Is their discomfort related to:
➤ Individual needs?
➤ Gender, e.g. a female being uncomfortable being asked to work physically with a male, or vice versa?
➤ Expectations/confusion – insufficient preparation?

Remember that inclusive sessions are not always appropriate for all participants at a given point in time.

Example

I was recently co-leading dance sessions with another experienced dance artist. We were working with a group of 12–20 teenagers who had all been out of mainstream education for varying lengths of time and for different reasons, ranging from purely medical to long-term psychiatric problems. The participants came from four different centres to a central venue, and most did not know each other.

One small group of girls who attended all had severe eating disorders and associated psychological problems. They would not join in, but sat on the outskirts of the sessions and were very withdrawn. We designed sessions to meet the needs of this group e.g. high and low impact options within each activity, physically setting the room out so that no-one felt 'watched', and providing individual attention. During one session my co-leader spent all her time enticing them into the activity, all with little result. A consequence of the amount of energy and focus going into that small group was that the other individuals' needs were not as well met at that time.

Assessing the situation with the dancers and staff, we all agreed that inclusive sessions were not relevant for most of those girls at that time. They were not ready to be integrated into a bigger group and we, as leaders, were not able to spend enough time to support them throughout the session. We arranged separate sessions with this group at their own centre, and work was successfully developed.

Are you ready to lead inclusive sessions?

Assess your own abilities honestly before you start to run inclusive sessions. You may need to increase your knowledge and skills before you embark on inclusive sessions.

You may need:
➤ more knowledge of specific disabilities,
➤ a wider experience of dance skills,
➤ more experience in facilitating sessions.

5

SUMMARY POINTS

➤ *Know* the needs of your group.

➤ *Prepare*:
 Yourself – clear objectives and inclusive ways of working;
 Support workers – clear understanding of their roles;
 Venue – fully accessible;
 Groups – introduce dance material and ways of working you will use.

➤ *Ensure* communication is appropriate for all dancers.

➤ *Ensure* dance work is challenging, enjoyable, accessible and a creative experience for all dancers.

➤ *Look out* for dancers who feel uncomfortable within a session, and assess why.

➤ *Explore and enjoy* the creative potential and possibilities that differences within a group can offer.

➤ *Aim* for high quality work.

5

63

Tomorrow's dance makers

Developing young choreographers

Choreography is the art of composing dances – the process of generating, refining, selecting and ordering dance moves to create a whole dance piece.

What makes a young choreographer?

➤ Someone who is able to create dance – from initial gestures to developing whole phrases – as opposed to someone who purely follows instructions.

➤ Someone who is able to shape dance pieces and has an aesthetic awareness.

➤ Someone who understands that there are different ways of doing things and makes decisions. For some people decisions can be between stillness and movement. These choices can be a result of a spontaneous decision from within, rather than a response to a set of options given by a leader.

Joy of dancing

An enjoyment of dance for all involved – leader, dancers and support staff – should be the main thread running through dance sessions. When introducing choreographic devices and terminology, be careful not to lose the spirit of adventure and exploration that make dance a creative activity. Choreographic devices are useful to have to refer to, reflect on and have fun with.

Be careful not to lose the spirit of adventure and exploration that make dance a creative activity

6

65

Watching for starting points

There are many ways of initiating dance pieces. Often the dancers themselves will indicate (either verbally or non-verbally) an appropriate initial starting point. Look for the dance potential in any situation. Using dancers' input is vital for them to feel that their contributions are valued.

**Look for the dance
potential in any situation**

Example

I was working with a group of teenagers who had been out of mainstream schools for long periods of time for a number of reasons, both medical and psychiatric. The group met and worked with me in a dance studio, which was a new space for them.

On our first meeting the group walked into the room and almost all of them sat or stood behind and leant on chairs that had been left in the corner of the studio from the previous evening. The chairs seemed to be providing a safety barrier. So we worked using the chairs throughout the warm up and experimented with how we could use the chairs to move on, around, over, under, away from, skid on, lift and how they could define relationships. This led to duet work, and further group choreography. Over a period of weeks they devised a whole piece, to music they selected.

Finding spontaneity in a pre-determined theme

If you are working to a pre-determined theme you can still encourage use of imagination and exploration to gain original creative outcomes.

Example

I was given the theme of a big stone boulder to devise a piece of dance with 14 children. We started with a word brainstorm, and then built dance phrases using some of their words, such as *twisted, straight, looped* and *heavy load*.

The whole piece was based on them devising shapes and dance phrases which travelled, repeated, built in momentum and speed, varied in direction and volume of dancers – but all based on those five words.

Even if a theme is set, the dancers can still direct the piece by:

➤ Re-defining the theme – their responses to and thoughts about the given theme.

➤ Creating dance material – devising dance phrases based on their words, thoughts and images.

➤ Shaping and ordering dance material – making choreographic choices and decisions.

➤ Reflecting and adapting dance material – assessing the piece of dance and developing analytical and critical opinions. Making changes and adaptations as a result of these.

Being a navigator

As material is being developed, you as session leader act as the navigator. You are ultimately responsible for the route. Sometimes you can see the way ahead and you will know certain avenues will lead to dead ends. Sometimes there is a choice of routes. At times you are as lost as everyone else. And just sometimes you know the quickest route and need to use it due to time constraints!

Providing choices

Throughout sessions, present your group with choices. The choice may sometimes be as open as 'What happens next?'. At other times you may give the group two or three options.

To reach a decision, discuss the possibilities and either:
➤ take a group consensus, or
➤ identify a person or small group to make the decision.

Choices may be related to the content of the session, e.g. 'How shall we end the session today?'. They may be related to the development of a dance piece, e.g. 'How do you want the piece to end?'.

Seizing the moment

For dancers who do not have the cognitive ability to recall and remember, dances take place 'in the moment'. Any spontaneous movement or dance will be using choreographic devices such as use of space, speed, repetition of single movements or phrases of movements, and use of dance actions. These will not be pre-planned and discussed but will just flow through the dancer's body at that point in time. These dances, which may be only seconds long, are of equal value to rehearsed pieces.

Moving together

Spontaneous dances, which may only be seconds long, are of equal value to rehearsed pieces

The role of support workers

Be clear on the role of support workers in the session. Do you want support workers to be:
➤ co-dancers – an equal partnership between dancer and support worker?
➤ enablers – responding to dancers' cues (verbal or non-verbal)?
➤ almost invisible – e.g. a member of staff moving a wheelchair, but the key focus is the dancer in the wheelchair?

6

67

It is vital that you are clear which role staff are taking and share this information with them, so that there is a common understanding between all staff in the session. Staff may need training prior to the dance sessions, to discuss and explore their role and ways of working within dance sessions.

Building your choreographic knowledge

➤ Watch dance work – the more you see, the more you will begin to compare and contrast pieces.

Consider especially:

  ➤ accompaniments to dance pieces – music/sound/set/projection,
  ➤ shape of pieces,
  ➤ theme of pieces,
  ➤ the positioning of dancers and their relationship to each other,
  ➤ use of space, i.e. is the performing space a vast space or small? How do the dancers move within it?
  ➤ use of choreographic devices such as speed, rhythm, differing levels, canon, unison, repetition, group formations, etc.

➤ Watch TV programmes about dance – many have interviews with choreographers and dancers talking about their work.

➤ Training – pursue training opportunities via education and dance/ arts organisations (see *Useful addresses* on page 122).

➤ Books – there are some useful books about individual dance styles and choreographers (see *Further reading* on page 121).

➤ Be aware of choreographic potential in everyday life, e.g. people's gestures, photographs. A selection of photographs with clear body shapes can be sequenced. Dancers copy the shapes in sequence to create a basic phrase of movements that can then be developed.

Developing dancers' choreographic knowledge

➤ Use choreographic terms within sessions, e.g. unison, canon, etc. and explain what they mean (see *Glossary* on page 124). Then explore these devices.

➤ Use video clips of professional dance pieces and of the dance group's work to identify and consider choreography.

➤ Use the language of dance and choreographic terms when analysing and reflecting on work.

➤ Watch and reflect on each other's work – encourage questions.

6

Example

When performing dances, ask the dancers to consider:

➤ How does it feel to perform the piece?

➤ Do different sections or movements prompt particular feelings or images?

➤ Are you aware of patterns and relationships with other dancers when you perform the piece?

When watching dance, ask questions to help build an awareness of dance/movement and choreography, such as:

➤ How many dancers are dancing at any one time?

➤ Where are they dancing in the space?

➤ What patterns or shapes do you see?

➤ Describe the movement you see.

➤ How do you feel when watching?

➤ Do you see a variety of movements, speeds, levels, shapes, dynamics?

➤ What don't you see?

➤ What does the dance make you think of? Consider words, images, feelings, colours, physical response (a still position can initiate a response in a way words cannot).

What patterns or shapes do you see?

The participants in your dance session will each have ideas, ways of moving and responses that, however small and maybe infrequent, are valuable contributions. In my experience, the ideal dance session is one of co-dancers with a navigator, who helps to find and travel the most adventurous route to dance making.

6

SUMMARY POINTS

➤ *Ask* questions that require factual, descriptive, interpretative and opinion-based answers (these do not need to be verbal).

➤ *Encourage* dancers' input – movement material, choreographic ideas, feedback, etc.

➤ *Be flexible* – in approach, session format, etc. Be wary of holding too many set ideas of outcomes.

➤ *Support workers* need to be clear of their role within sessions.

➤ *Reflect* – give time for reflection (verbal or otherwise), watching, moving and thinking.

➤ At the end of a session, *ask yourself:* Whose work is it – mine, theirs or ours?

Show and tell

Ways of sharing work

Dance work is most commonly linked with performance. Within the national curriculum, performance is identified as one of the key elements to be experienced within dance. However, my experience is that young people and adults who have been outside the mainstream for long periods of time often find the idea of performing live a distressing and frightening prospect. In such cases, expecting them to perform in front of an audience may be a self-defeating exercise. However, project funders, governors, the school assembly or an annual Christmas show can sometimes present a situation where you are required to contribute dance work.

A piece of work is performed

In any situation, if work is of a good quality and/or of significance, then performing in public can be an extremely valuable exercise for the performers (in terms of self-confidence and being seen and valued), and for the profile of the work. In some instances a performance at the end of a series of sessions can provide a focus, and possibly kudos to the work.

This chapter suggests a variety of ways of sharing work.

The context for sharing

There are many contexts in which sharing of work can take place:

Within a session

The dancers witness and watch other groups sharing the work produced within sessions. This may be spontaneous work that lasts for a few seconds and can never be repeated, or the beginnings of a longer piece of specific performance work to be further rehearsed and developed. Watching others work can lead to a sharing of ideas, and also to appraisals, giving pupils the opportunity to be choreographers and dance critics.

Across a project

Groups who have been working alone come together to show their work. These may be groups working in different art forms but with a similar starting point, or groups whose pieces link together in some way.

Performance

Individuals/groups come together to perform pieces as part of a larger performance or festival.

When to share

Sharings and performances can take place at different times during an initiative or project.

Initial responses

Individuals/groups present their initial dance and movement responses in order to generate a range of material for the group to select from and develop further.

Work in progress

Work that is past the initial stages but not in a final state for a formal performance. Feedback from viewers may be welcomed at this point, and comments may influence further work.

Performance

Work that has been created and developed to be viewed.

What to call the event

The purpose of the sharing or performance will dictate the tone of the event. Name your event with care as it will project the purpose and meaning of it. If people are expecting a peformance and are actually attending an informal work in progress, expectations and reality are mismatched before anyone has danced at all!

Informal and formal showings can be called:

Showing   Sharing   Work in progress

          Presentation   Performance   Informal viewing

Preview   Demonstration   Production

          Spectacle   Display   Forum   Open workshop

Reasons for showing work

Representing and showing dance work can be important in many ways, such as:

➤ *informing and educating people* – parents, colleagues, other children/adults in an establishment, governors, decision makers, local government officers, councillors, funders;
➤ *profiling dance work* within an establishment, Local Education Authority, region, etc;
➤ *enabling performers to be seen in a different way* to their normal existence within an establishment or organisation;
➤ *challenging people's perceptions* of dance and/or the dancers;
➤ *enabling people to succeed* (performers and creators);
➤ *expressing thoughts, images, messages* that are important to those who created the piece and/or the audience;
➤ *allowing dancers to experience performing* and being seen and valued;
➤ *illustrating cross-arts projects* and cross curricula links;
➤ *disseminating ideas* or ways of working;
➤ *celebrating a particular moment*, event or achievement.

Deciding how to show work

There are different ways of showing work and these can be combined in a variety of ways.

How you show work will depend on:
➤ the purpose of showing work,

Sharing work in a session

7

73

➤ the group you are working with (their needs and desires),
➤ the venue,
➤ the context of the showing,
➤ logistics and practicalities (such as budget!).

I often work with groups or individuals for whom performing on a stage is an impossibility or extremely distressing. However, I have needed to find ways of showing their work and ensuring it is seen and valued alongside live performance work.

The next sections present various ways of showing dance work. I have used them all, at various times, and in different combinations. Each has its positive and negative points.

Slides

Remember to obtain permission to photograph the dancers (see *Practical and logistical points to remember* on page 3).

You can use slide film to capture key moments and images that communicate the creativity, achievements and artistry of the individual/ group. I tend to show the slides with no verbal commentary (after a verbal introduction), and accompanied by music (possibly something that has been used in sessions, or that captures the energy and spirit of the sessions). This becomes a presentation in its own right, with a multi-sensory approach, i.e. lowered lights, music, selected visual images.

A digital camera can be used to take images that are then formatted into a PowerPoint presentation. A combination of images, music and text are possible in this format.

Positive points
➤ If the images are of a good enough quality and really capture key moments, they can be a powerful way of presenting the essence of dance work.
➤ The 'frozen moments in time' that images produce are powerful as they provide a sharp focus for the viewer.
➤ Combining the images with music creates a multi-sensory presentation and so has a bigger impact on the viewer/listener.
➤ By selecting the images you/the group have control over what the audience sees.

7

74

Negative points
➤ The images need to be of very good quality.
➤ You need to take the photographs in a well lit space. If you have to change venue to do this, it may upset the balance of some groups/individuals, which can then impact onto the dance session.
➤ The 'magic moments' can be hard to capture quickly enough and you have to decide whether to re-run or set up a photo shoot. You may need to set up a separate photo shoot in order to avoid the flow of a dance session being altered and interrupted by photography. A photo shoot has a different objective and can be a different and valuable experience for dancers.
➤ There is no live element to the presentation.

Photographs
Remember to obtain permission to photograph the dancers (see *Practical and logistical points to remember* on page 3).

As with slides, photographs can be a way of presenting moments and highlights from dance sessions. You need to decide whether you want digital prints, more traditional prints, black and white, or colour, and what size the prints need to be for easy viewing.

Positive points
➤ Once the photographs have been processed, selected and mounted, the exhibition can exist for a long period of time, and even tour without anyone being required to operate equipment.
➤ People can spend as much time as they need examining and considering each image – moving on at their own speed.
➤ An exhibition can tour widely, and therefore have a wide geographic profile.
➤ Written captions can put an image into context, or focus or challenge the viewer.
➤ Photographs can last for a long time.
➤ Photographs can serve as a record/memento of work for individuals. They can be used as 'evidence' of dancers' individual learning targets.

Negative points
As for slides.

Setting up a photo shoot

➤ An obtrusive and insensitive photographer can impact on the confidence and self-image of dancers. The photo shoot must be run by someone who knows the dancers and the dance work well (e.g. session leader), and can act as a broker between dancers and photographer.

➤ Care must be taken around the physical handling of dancers (especially those with physical disabilities) when posing people for photographs.

➤ You will need a warm up before the photographs are taken. Dancers must be physically warm before holding positions for any length of time.

Video

Remember to obtain permission to video the dancers (see *Practical and logistical points to remember* on page 3).

The video can be choreographed and edited to present the moving images in the order and way that you and the group wish. If a dance piece is being choreographed for film, then you need to think of the editing as part of the choreographic process. The advantage of editing is that you are drawing the eye of the viewer to specific foci. For example, you can use:

➤ close ups,

➤ group shots,

➤ the camera to move across the group of dancers.

Positive points

➤ You can re-run the dance and keep the 'best' run as the final performance. You don't have only one chance, as in a live performance.

➤ Performers have a chance to watch themselves, and develop their appraisal skills.

➤ Copies can be made easily for each performer at a low cost.

➤ Videos can be sent to a group or individual for viewing when convenient, so do not rely on someone being able to make a particular date, time and venue for a performance.

➤ Videos can be shown at a wide range of small-scale venues from private homes to school halls and do not rely on highly specialised equipment.

➤ Videos last a long time.

The video can be choreographed and edited to present the moving images in the order and way that you and the group wish

➤ Videos can create a record for choreographers, can be used to re-create work, and as evidence of work achieved, etc.

Negative points
➤ Video can give a 'removed' and distanced view of live dance.
➤ Post-production editing can be time-consuming and costly.
➤ It is relatively costly or requires specialised equipment to show videos on a large screen in a big venue.

Digital video
Remember to obtain permission to video the dancers (see *Practical and logistical points to remember* on page 3).

The main drawback of using this is the expense of the equipment and the expertise needed. However, if the budget allows, digital projection can mean that you can project on to anything, such as the side of a building.

If you have a project involving a digital artist, it may be worth investigating the possibilities in order to create a 'one-off' projection event that uses an unusual and large scale backdrop – e.g. a playground, a wall, a roof, the water in a swimming pool.

Open workshop – work in progress
Inviting small numbers of people to view, or preferably take part in a workshop, can allow people to experience live dance within a specific setting. It may be helpful to run a briefing session for guests beforehand (see negative points below).

Positive points
➤ If invited guests join in, the dancers may be at an advantage in being more familiar and experienced within dance workshops. This can give dancers control and opportunities to be 'in the driving seat'.
➤ The usual venue, formats and structures can be used, which may be reassuring and familiar for participants. Therefore the dance work does not suffer.
➤ Guests can witness a 'real' (as possible) dance workshop, rather than edited highlights or rehearsed pieces.
➤ Specific processes can be used, demonstrating to guests good working practice or a specific way of working.

7

77

Open workshops allow guests to experience live dance

Negative points

➤ Any unfamiliar face can upset the balance of some groups.

➤ Guests who are unwilling to participate may create an awkward atmosphere. (Briefing prior to a session may avoid this.)

➤ Guests may make inappropriate comments or suggestions during a session that you may need to respond to. (Briefing prior to a session may avoid this.)

➤ The guests will see everything – not the edited highlights. If sessions are unpredictable, this may be a problem.

➤ If the group or an individual have unpredictable and physically challenging behaviour, guests unused to this may focus on this behaviour, rather than the content of the sessions and other dancers' involvement. (Briefing prior to a session may avoid this.)

➤ As leader you may not be ready and comfortable to work this way.

Live performance

While other ways of showing work create interesting ideas, none can recreate the immediacy and intimacy of a live performance.

Positive points

➤ Performers and audience are both within the same experience in terms of place and time. This is the unique experience of live performance.

➤ The performers get live feedback and recognition from the audience.

➤ The 'once only' chance performers have for the performance creates an exciting and sometimes fragile edge to the piece.

Sharing ideas via performance within a session

➤ Adrenalin and nerves can be great aides to heighten a performance or paralysing obstacles. Live performances can create the chance to learn to control and manage nerves – a useful skill for life generally!

➤ Working towards a performance can provide a focus to the process that helps to 'drive the piece on'.

Negative points

➤ The 'once only' chance can create great pressure on those involved with the performance. People with unpredictable and/or challenging behaviour can create an extra pressure, and the focus of the performance may become containment of behaviour.

➤ A 'once only' chance may be unrealistic for some performers who need more time/tries. However, you can structure the performance to accommodate this.

➤ Live performance can create time deadlines. Cues for 'changing places or costumes', etc. can create complicated logistical scenarios. However, a performance can be structured to eliminate these.

Pick and mix

Combinations of different ways of showing work may work well. For example:

➤ An exhibition of photographs and events leading up to a final live performance.

➤ Live dance with projections on to the dancers and/or backdrop.

➤ An open-workshop/informal performance that involves the audience taking part in some way.

Informing others about work done

Accounts of work in progress, forthcoming and existing projects or critical accounts of performances can all be communicated in many ways including:

➤ exhibitions in school, feeder schools/centres, local library, day centres, etc.

➤ newsletters,

➤ speech in school assembly.

Keeping people such as parents, governors, decision-makers and funders informed of the dance that is taking place can be vital in terms of:

➤ creating a culture where the arts in general and dance in particular are important, valued and noted;

➤ profiling activity to create a known track record of work that may be relevant for future funding initiatives or opportunities. Funders may need evidence of past work or a portfolio that proves the worth of work to date.

SUMMARY POINTS

➤ *Be clear* what the reasons are for showing dance work.

➤ *Think* of creative ways of showing and sharing work.

➤ *Select* a way of showing work that is appropriate to the dancers and the audience, and that gives them a high quality experience of dance work.

➤ *Ensure* that you as leader are comfortable with the chosen way of showing work.

➤ *Support workers* need to be clear about and comfortable with their role within the sharing of work.

➤ *Prepare* your dancers – ensure they are clear about what is going to happen.

➤ *Prepare* your audience – publicise your event clearly, giving the audience clear expectations.

7

A bag of tricks?

Using props within dance sessions

When starting dance sessions with people with disabilities, many people feel that they need to use props, perhaps because of an assumption that whatever movement a person with disabilities has, it will not be enough in itself to constitute 'dance'. Also, individuals may respond particularly well to a specific stimulus e.g. fabric, which may provide a good starting point for practical dance work.

Having seen many people enjoy using props during sessions I do know they can be a successful starting point. However, I feel strongly that any group has ample movement and dance potential within it, regardless of props, and it is too easy to leave our natural movement vocabulary untapped and discount it in preference for external props. *A balance is the ideal.* Props are great as a starting point, and as a spark for dance ideas and movement responses, which can then take over as the content of a session. Props can also be great fun and encourage a climate of exploration and playfulness, but always remember that *props should enhance movement, not mask it.*

Props can be fun and encourage exploration

Some of the factors to consider before deciding whether to introduce props into a session are given in the table on page 82.

8

81

Positive factors	But...
Props can extend and magnify small movements.	Small movement is valid and should stand alone.
Props can introduce variety and 'difference' to a session.	Everybody moves differently; this variety can be celebrated and used within a session.
Props can distract someone who feels self-conscious or antagonistic about dancing.	Props can be used as potential weapons, or be destroyed and so cause distractions.
Props can bring a multi-sensory dimension to a session, introducing sound, touch and visual elements.	Props may cause handling challenges to a group or be destroyed through over enthusiastic touching, holding, feeling and mouthing. Dancers can concentrate on the prop rather than dancing with it.
Props can create a visual spectacle, which can be pleasing to dancer and audience.	Smaller movement is valid and needs to be 'seen' and appreciated too.
Props can create an immediate shared starting point for a group.	Our bodies are, in themselves, the initial starting point for any interaction – we are all constantly moving and interacting non-verbally.
Props can be used as a barrier in partner work in a positive way – allowing connection without direct contact.	Props can be used as a barrier in partner work in a negative way – dancers relating to the prop rather than to each other.

More positive reasons for using props

➤ Props can make physical links between individual group members, therefore creating a 'sense' of the group.

Props can create a 'sense' of 'group'

➤ Props can enable people to assume different identities and experiment with movements and dynamics that are not their usual familiar ones.

➤ Large material can create a hidden safe place for movements to be practised unseen – this could be just one body part, e.g. hands and fingers or feet.

Example

Some university students I was working with were on placement in a special school. One student noticed a child who said and contributed little within sessions, but her fingers were moving under a piece of lycra. Her movements were progressively getting larger, more complicated and more confident. The student asked her if they could all try her finger and hand movements. These became the starting point for a piece of dance for the whole group. The child had been using the lycra as a safe space to experiment.

Using the child's own toy as an ice-breaker for partner work

Deciding whether to use props

If you consider *why* you wish to use props in a particular session, this may help clarify *how* you might use them in that session.

Example

Working in a hospital ward setting, it can be invaluable to use a child's own toy or belonging as a starting point for conversation, and then using the object either as a stimulus for dance work or as a prop. In this way the prop acts as an ice-breaker, and an external common starting point.

Using ribbons

Tried and tested props

These items are used regularly by many teachers and dance practitioners:

➤ ribbons and ribbon sticks,

➤ elastics,

➤ fabric – large pieces of stretchy lycra, small squares of different weighted, coloured and textured fabrics, large parachute-type material,

➤ sticks of different widths and lengths,

➤ toys – expanding and retracting balls, clockwork moving figures, marionette-type figures,

Working with fabric

8

83

- feathers – large and small,
- hats in a variety of sizes, styles, etc,
- scarves in a variety of lengths, weights, textures,
- balls – spongy and soft, hard, with bells inside, light balloon types,
- shoes – which can be used to make sounds. They can be worn on the hands, so being unable to use the feet should be no barrier.

Learning objectives

How you use the prop will depend on your learning objectives for the session. The objectives listed below relate specifically to props.

- To enhance a particular movement dynamic or aspect of dance work, such as partner work.
- To encourage creative exploration through movement and prompt natural responses rather than 'learned' dance material.
- To reassure you as a leader whilst you get to know your group.
- To create a fun, 'external' starting point.
- To add variety, particularly for those with limited movement such as quadriplegics. For example, blowing through straws to move balloons, or using the head to echo the shapes a partner makes with a ribbon.

Getting started

You will still need a warm up activity, to ensure that bodies are awake, alert, warm and therefore safe. You may wish to include the prop within the warm up.

Example

The prop can be passed around the circle and each person can show a movement in response to the prop. You will need to be watching intently, in order to see even the smallest reaction.

The rest of the group can then try that movement (without holding the prop), i.e. using only the pure movement, extracted from the prop. For example, if someone lifts the object up to look at the light through it, the group will echo this, raising arms and heads.

After a warm up you may wish to remove the prop and concentrate on the movements that were generated. You could then develop small dances by including all/some/one of the

Working with straws

movements (and then vary them). (See *Tomorrow's dance makers* on page 65.)

Another way of using props is to introduce the object to aid a specific point.

> **Example**
> When dancers are working in pairs, echoing and mirroring movements, you can encourage delicate and accurate movement by giving them straws to work with. They experiment using different movements without dropping the straw. The straws will help to magnify the non-verbal relationship between partners.

Exploring props

Watch for the dancers' instinctive and natural movement responses to props that you introduce – these may be different from your own ideas. Try them.

➤ How can you use the prop when dancing:
  ➤ alone,
  ➤ with a partner,
  ➤ in a small group,
  ➤ in a large group?
➤ Does the prop make a sound when it is moving? Can you make other sounds with the prop? Try shaking, tapping, etc.

Exploring props

➤ Can your prop travel:
  ➤ as high as possible,
  ➤ as low as possible,
  ➤ against different surfaces – floor, someone's back, etc?
➤ Consider the way the prop moves. How many different ways can it move? For example, a ball rolls, bounces, spins, can be squeezed, held still, etc.

8

85

Props as a sensory input

Props can provide sensory experiences within a dance session.

➤ Smell – use lightly scented oils or perfumes on scarves, fabrics, etc. Seek advice from a qualified aromatherapist and check with staff before using any essential oil. Avoid direct skin contact with oils and perfumes.

➤ Touch – use fabrics with differing textures, brushes or balls. Dancers can lie underneath a parachute and feel the movement of the air as the fabric is lifted up and down.

➤ Sound – fabrics or ribbons that crinkle or rattle as they are moved using different body parts; instruments that can be a focal part of a dance, or can be danced with, e.g. shakers, sticks.

➤ Visual – lengths of fabric, e.g. ribbons or larger sheets of material to move around the space e.g. waft, drag, ripple; fabric to wrap people or parts of bodies in, to create different images.

Using fabric as a multi-sensory stimulus

Removing the prop

You also need to consider at what point you will remove the prop. Individuals can become very attached (metaphorically and physically!) to objects, the removal of which can then bring a session to a standstill.

A possible solution is to make the removal of the prop an activity in itself.

Example
➤ All letting go of a piece of fabric at the same time, watching it fall and settle.
➤ All throwing balls to one corner of the room or all passing them high, low, or in various ways to a bag or someone who puts them away.
➤ Arranging ribbons in a pattern on the floor that is then left in position as the group leaves the dance space.

SUMMARY POINTS

➤ *Consider* why you are using props in relation to your learning objectives. Which props are most appropriate to your learning objectives?

➤ *Explore* dance possibilities using props. Allow sufficient time for participants to really experiment.

➤ *Removing* the props – consider how and when you will do this.

➤ *Remember* that props should enhance dance movements, not mask them.

Dance in a wider context

Introduction

Dance can have different roles within a project, for example as a means of exploring ideas, or to create a polished performance piece. Dance can also be part of a project that has a far wider context than exploring dance as an art form.

This chapter presents two project case studies. These illustrate:
➤ contrasting roles that dance can play in a residency or project,
➤ contrasting ways that dance can combine with other art forms within a project,
➤ dance projects with different time scales,
➤ different aims and objectives and contrasting end products.

Both of these projects were designed and developed specifically to meet a defined brief in the agreed time scale and within the agreed budget. Each was designed to meet the needs of a particular group of dancers.

Case study: From space to place

A pilot project involving a dance artist and sculptor/photographer/ video-maker working with children and staff at two Warwickshire special schools (Marie Corelli and Lambert), which were being amalgamated into one special school (Welcombe Hills).

Brief: To work with pupils, staff and parents through practical arts workshops, to create a piece of public art that will feature in the new school building.

Outcome: A piece of 'public art' for the new school building.

Time scale:

September 2000 – January 2001	6 practical workshop days at primary site (including 1 day filming for the video)
June 2001	3 practical workshop days at secondary site (including 1 day filming for the video)
Artists' making time	9 days studio-based – glass-making/video editing

Opening of new building January 2003.

Participants: 3 classes from Primary school, 3 classes from Secondary school, staff and parents

Process: Participatory art workshops (dance, visual art, video and story telling) for staff, students and parents.

Role of dance: Dance was invaluable as a way for everyone to participate and contribute on an equal basis. Everyone had movements to offer.

First we needed a period of getting used to dancing and moving together. This was crucial to enable ways of working to develop where the students could be the decision makers – the choreographers.

88

Dance workshops

These explored themes of:

➤ *Changing spaces and boundaries*

Using elastics to create flexible, ever-changing boundaries to dance within and outside.

➤ *Mapping spaces*

Using tape on the hall floor to create routes around the space and mark out gathering points (inspired by the post-16 group's mappings of their class base).

➤ *Dens and special places*

Moving in, through and under marked spaces – marked by tape or created using material/parachutes. Experiencing being inside or outside dens. Viewing the environment from inside a safe space.

➤ *Journeys*

Creating routes and choreographing ways of moving along, negotiating others, passing, meeting, etc.

➤ *Turning*

This became a prevalent theme as the sculptural work progressed. A video camera was used to film students (from a range of classes) turning individually in any way they wished, e.g. a single body part turning, floor work, dancers in wheelchairs turning.

The final performance

The video was edited and projected as part of the opening ceremony for the new building and piece of public art in January 2003.

Split screen video still showing a child turning alongside a foil mould created in a visual arts session

9

Sunmoves was based at Sunfield – a residential care and education establishment in Clent, Worcestershire, that provides 52-week provision for young people aged 6–19 years with profound and severe learning needs. It also offers specialist provision for young people with autism.

Brief: To work alongside a land artist to develop the creative potential of Sunfield's grounds.

Outcome: Changes to the grounds that invite creative interaction.

Time scale:

| September 1998 – July 1999 | Pilot research (Year 1) |
| September 1999 – April 2001 | Design and construction (Year 2) |

Participants: Sunfield students, staff and families, local community, neighbouring schools.

Process: Participatory dance and visual/land art workshops with students, staff, families, local community, neighbouring schools.

Role of dance: Dance and movement were seen as essential to the project as a way of communicating and accessing the non-verbal students within Sunfield.

Dance workshops

In Year 1 these explored themes of:

➤ *Moving together*
  Using elastic to focus and bring a group of disparate young people together, devising circle dances.
➤ *Body awareness*
  Individual body parts, control, ability to alter levels, dynamics, speeds, etc. when dancing.
➤ *Exploring dynamics*
  High energy movements; slow, careful movements and stillness.
➤ *Developing relationships*
  Sharing space, echoing each individual's movements.

9

➤ *Ways of moving across spaces, from one place to another*
  Creating pathways and choreographing movement along them (see *Courtyard*, below).
➤ *Developing systems where students could be the decision-makers*
  Widget symbols (computer program) were a key resource, enabling non-verbal students to indicate movement and dance choices for the whole group to follow.
➤ *Following pathways – weaving*
  Developing a performance piece to celebrate the spaces.

Year 2 – interpreting the dance work

During the second year, Mike Fletcher, a land artist, joined the project. His role was to interpret the findings from the movement and dance sessions and translate these into landscape design.

As movement through space is a key feature of both choreography and landscape art, the art forms of dance and landscaping were crucial partners within Sunmoves. Mike Fletcher observed that, "If students could choreograph the direction, change speed and level within their movements …and make decisions about manipulating movement, they could also do this as part of a landscape project."

After a period of consultation and research with staff, students, the local community and the project advisory group, a series of proposals were developed. The final result is a series of structures that have transformed the potential of Sunfield's grounds.

Calm space

Calm space

This space includes an earth sculpture, which creates a haven of tranquillity and harnesses the natural sources of light and sound. A dry stone waller was commissioned to produce Mike Fletcher's design of a snaking wall, which creates a spiral boundary to the space. The space is surrounded by aspen trees, especially chosen for the whispering sound and reflective quality of the leaves. A chamomile carpet also adds a soothing scent and sense of calm to the space. A series of stepping stones (an idea originating from a dance piece developed with a local first school), help students find the space.

Courtyard
An area for meeting, greeting and travelling through, using the notion

9

of creative and fun ways of moving through a space. A winding concrete path is patterned using intuitive marks originally made by students in a visual art workshop. These marks include little runways – water can be poured down these and watched as it trickles along the pathway. This has been used as a resource for investigation as part of the science curriculum. A winding wall of oak provides a surface for seating or climbing and balancing. The space is surrounded by a number of trees that create areas of shade, define the boundary and change colour throughout the seasons from pale green leaves to vibrant red ones. The variety of textures and colours creates a very responsive environment.

Courtyard pathway

Driveway

A series of wooden sculptures create a walkway and can be used in a number of ways. The sculptures can be used purely as markers to create a rhythm and destination to move towards, or using a ball (or conker, stone, fir cone, etc.), each one can be used to discover the possibilities of rolling, balancing, and retrieving balls/objects as they travel along the inner or outer spirals. The texture and form of the carved wood can be explored by hands, and in some cases climbed.

Dance workshops explored body shapes and forms that a ball could be balanced or rolled on, under or through. These sessions were photographed and those images fed into the design process.

Sculpture and part of walkway

Willow works

The first initiative was to create a series of structures from living willow, e.g. domes and tunnels emerging from existing hedges. They were an experiment to see how students and staff might use structures that could provide:

➤ a feeling of close containment and possibly security,
➤ tunnels to run, roll and chase through,
➤ small domes to sit in and relax, contemplating the outdoor sensations – sights, sounds, feeling of breezes, etc.

The structures were enjoyed and enthusiastically embraced as a new outdoor resource. Further willow structures were commissioned and built in 1999, to create an area of 'willow works'. Shapes made from woven willow have also been used within the maths curriculum. A large dome within a dome was built as a possibility for an outdoor

Willow tunnel

classroom where a whole class could sit together.

How the spaces can be used

➤ As a curriculum-related learning resource, e.g. for growth cycles as the willow changes form through the seasons, for storytelling, circle time sessions in calm space, movement/dance sessions across the courtyard pathway, etc.

➤ As interactive spaces enabling students to negotiate the outdoor environment.

➤ As experiential spaces – natural sources and sensations (light, sound, colour, texture).

➤ As places to explore physically – climbing, balancing, running along curved surfaces, jumping, rolling and hovering along giant stepping stones.

Sunmoves provided an opportunity for many partnerships to be established. Events included: dance work with Belbroughton CE First School and Clent Parochial First School; visual art work with Haybridge High School; a Community Dance Group involving grandparents, parents and young people from Clent village.

The final performance

The culmination of Sunmoves was marked by a site specific dance and music performance in April 2001, involving professional dancers and musicians, Sunfield staff and students, local First School children and a Community Dance Group established as part of the project. They performed newly created dance pieces that echoed and celebrated the essence of each new space in the grounds. The event was attended by regional and local arts officers, parents, funders, members of the local community, Sunfield staff and students and was a vibrant and fitting celebration of the achievements to date.

9

93

Dance ideas

Introduction

The ideas and activities in this section are all tried and tested and have worked in a variety of settings.

The ideas provide a useful framework, but you will need to adapt the material so that it is appropriate for the individuals you are working with. They are not separated into categories such as age range, key stage, non-verbal participants, participants with limited movements, inclusive sessions, etc. Most of the ideas work at many levels but you will need to deliver them in a way that is appropriate to your group.

There are three dance ideas for warm ups, four for the main part of a lesson, and three for relaxation at the end of the lesson. (See *Further reading* on page 121 for other books containing dance ideas.)

Read	the ideas
Imagine	how they can work
Select	what appeals to you
Experiment	and try ideas out
Adapt	as you wish
ENJOY	

10

95

Warm up
Group dances

Group activity

Equipment needed: none

Activity
Seated, standing or lying in a circle the group decides on three or four movements that they link together into a phrase.

Allow time to practise and repeat movements until everyone is happy. You may wish to play some music, such as a jig or a reel for people to respond to. The phrase can be performed with music and repeated as many times as wished.

Developments
➤ Create ways of turning as a group, with partners or individually, and then repeat your initial phrase again.
➤ Vary your initial phrase by:
  ➤ changing the speed of movements,
  ➤ changing the size of movements,
  ➤ performing the movements at a high or low level,
  ➤ working with a partner to incorporate physical contact and/ or ways of making the moves into a duet, e.g. facing each other, dancing towards, around and away from each other.
➤ Create a new phrase of four different movements that can link together.
➤ Create ways of travelling, as a group, to a new space in your hall to start your dance all over again.
➤ Vary your phrases by introducing specific challenges, e.g. everyone lying down, only using shoulders, all seated.

Ways of turning as a group

Remember
➤ The smallest movement, and still positions, are valid contributions and can be part of a dance.
➤ Do not be afraid to repeat the dance. People can enjoy a familiar structure and become confident and more relaxed.

10

Dance/choreographic skills involved

➤ Contributing movement ideas
➤ Building movement phrases into a repeatable structure
➤ Spatial awareness
➤ Dancing within a group
➤ Movement memory

Personal/group skills involved

➤ Working within a group – awareness of others
➤ Memory
➤ Negotiation
➤ Ability to contribute ideas
➤ Creativity

Warm up
Body parts

Partner work/group activity

Equipment needed: none

Activity 1

Identify different body parts, either verbally (by naming) or non-verbally (by physically touching).

In pairs, connect a body part with your partner's, e.g. elbows. Explore how these can move and remain connected, e.g. wiggle, circle, sway, press, rise, fall.

Connecting feet

Vary the:
➤ speed
➤ rhythm
➤ size
➤ length
➤ dynamic of movements
➤ level of the movements

Introduce moments of stillness.

Link movements that connect different body parts, e.g. feet connected followed by ears connected.

Activity 2

Start with a steady rhythm, either from CD/tape or dancers clapping or stamping.

A designated 'caller' shouts out a body part and the partners have to ensure that those body parts are touching, keeping to the rhythm established.

Example			
clap	clap	clap	KNEES
wait	wait	wait	SHOULDERS

- ➤ Vary the activity by shouting two body parts, e.g. foot and shoulder. Partners then have to ensure those two body parts are touching.
- ➤ Develop a group activity. The caller shouts a collection of body parts, e.g. 3 feet, 1 shoulder, 2 elbows, 1 back and a head! Dancers have to get into small groups and negotiate a 'collection' of those body parts that are somehow touching or physically connected.
- ➤ Encourage participants to work non-verbally and to negotiate non-verbally, i.e. not instructing each other verbally, but physically improvising and responding to each other.

Note the unusual shapes that partners and groups are making by naturally using different levels to connect body parts.

Remember
- ➤ This activity requires people to be comfortable about touching, and being touched by someone else.
- ➤ If physical contact is involved, check that all the dancers' physical management programmes include this.
- ➤ Some medical conditions may prohibit sudden physical contact – seek advice.
- ➤ Care is needed and all dancers must be aware of how to make physical contact carefully and safely.

Dance/choreographic skills involved
- ➤ Use of levels – high, medium, low/floor level
- ➤ Improvisation
- ➤ Partner work
- ➤ Small group work
- ➤ Development of rhythm

Personal/group skills involved
- ➤ Partner work – co-operation
- ➤ Small group work
- ➤ Responding to instructions
- ➤ Problem solving
- ➤ Non-verbal negotiation

10

99

Individual/partner work

Equipment needed: none

In all these activities, encourage the dancers to work non-verbally, physically improvising and responding to each other.

Activity 1
Working at any level – sitting, standing or lying – explore how many different ways you can stretch:
➤ with different body parts leading, e.g. chin, elbows, knees,
➤ in different directions, e.g. up, down, behind,
➤ with different dynamics, e.g. smoothly, sharply,
➤ at different speeds, e.g. fast, slow, combinations of fast to slow,
➤ on different levels, e.g. high, low, medium height.

Link stretches with other movements, e.g. stretch–turn–stretch–turn.

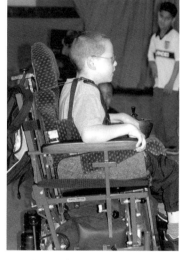

Stretching different body parts

Activity 2
Working with a partner:
➤ mirror (copy) each other's stretches,
➤ restrict the space, e.g. stay close to your partner, both stretching in your own time and your own way,
➤ find ways of stretching together, maintaining physical contact at all times, e.g. palms of hands together, shoulders together.

Activity 3
Choose a surface, e.g. wall, floor. Work on your own or with a partner.
➤ Keeping two or three body parts in contact with the chosen surface at all times, explore ways of stretching away from the surface.
➤ Change the body parts in contact with the surface, e.g. hands and feet, knees and hands, back and arms.

Stretching with a partner

Stretching with hoops

Activity 4

Use an object such as a chair or hoop and find ways of stretching away from it.

➤ Vary the body part that is leading.

➤ Work with a partner to find contrasting ways of stretching away from the object.

Remember

➤ This activity requires people to be comfortable about touching, and being touched by someone else.

➤ If physical contact is involved, check that all the dancers' physical management programmes include this.

➤ Some medical conditions may prohibit sudden physical contact – seek advice.

➤ Care is needed and all dancers must be aware of how to make physical contact carefully and safely.

➤ Each individual will have his or her own maximum stretch, which will be different from other people's.

➤ Encourage dancers to stretch to their maximum. They should not compete with each other, but could try to improve their own previous best or most imaginative/creative stretch.

Dance/choreographic skills involved

➤ Use of levels – high, medium, low/floor level

➤ Improvisation

➤ Partner work

➤ Use of dynamics

➤ Use of speed

➤ Linking movements and developing phrases

➤ Exploring the concept of stretching

Personal/group skills involved

➤ Partner work – co-operation

➤ Responding to instructions

➤ Problem solving

➤ Non-verbal negotiation

➤ Improvisation

➤ Exploring movements related to the word 'stretch'

10

101

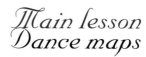

Main lesson
Dance maps

Individual or small group work

Equipment needed: masking tape or chalk

Activity 1
Designing the pathway

The dancers should work in small groups, in pairs, or one-to-one with a support worker.

➤ Give each group/pair a starting point and a finishing point within the space, e.g. start by the wall bars and finish by windows on the opposite side of the room.

➤ The groups/pairs then plan a pathway they wish people to take, i.e. *Where* do they want people to travel? The pathways cannot be just one straight line. You may need to explore options such as curvy lines, circles, loops, zigzags.

➤ Experiment with varying the size and frequency of the shapes along a pathway.

➤ The groups/pairs mark their pathway using masking tape or chalk.

➤ Groups/pairs walk the pathway to make sure they are happy with it, and make any necessary alterations.

➤ Different groups' pathways may cross each other. This if fine – you may want to encourage this.

Choreographing the movement

➤ Next the groups/pairs decide *how* they want people to travel along their pathway.

➤ Stick paper signs to different parts of the pathway on the floor, giving instructions on how to move. These can be can be adapted to a dancer's preferred method of communication, e.g. symbols, words, pictures.

➤ Ensure that the pathways are not over-signposted.
➤ Ensure that signs/instructions allow a certain amount of improvisation and interpretation by the traveller. For example, use the sign "fast turns", *not* "fast turns starting on right foot with arms above head and ..."

Dancing the pathways

All the dancers can explore the pathways.

In order to control the flow of bodies you may want to introduce different options, for example:

➤ you can jump from one pathway to another without completing it;
➤ you freeze when you meet someone and negotiate passing in slow motion;
➤ take time out to watch others moving along pathways;
➤ restrict the number of participants on pathways at any one time.

Adding music will influence the way the dancers move and respond. Experiment with music with different styles, cultural influences and instruments.

Encourage participants to improvise and work non-verbally, rather than planning and pre-practising movements.

Remember

➤ Over-complicated pathway designs or instructions will make the activity difficult and fractured.
➤ Ensure that dancers have an opportunity to watch others using pathways and interpreting movement instructions.
➤ Ensure that pathways are designed by and for wheelchair users,

10

e.g. tight loops may not be possible for wheelchairs.

Dance/choreographic skills involved
➤ Improvising
➤ Spatial awareness
➤ Exploring movement ideas
➤ Working as part of an overall group
➤ Working non-verbally

Personal/group skills involved
➤ Decision making
➤ Co-operation
➤ Improvising
➤ Imagination
➤ Use of space
➤ Working within a structure
➤ Working non-verbally

Main lesson
The immediate environment

Group and/or partner work

Equipment needed: cushions, lighting gel, coloured light bulbs, torches, materials in a variety of textures, foil, etc.

Activity 1
Using objects that are to hand can be crucial in developing movement relationships, particularly in one-to-one settings such as a hospital ward.

What can we do a cushion?
➤ Squeeze it with hands, elbows, feet, etc.
➤ Hug it – quick hug, big slow motion hug, swaying hug.
➤ Throw it upwards, at something, to each other, dodge the cushion, spin it in the air.
➤ Pass it to each other high, low, between feet, elbows, hold it between our backs.
➤ Balance on head (or on other body parts), find ways of travelling with it on the head, turning with it on the head.
➤ Remove the cushion and try the above activities again, i.e. passing an imaginary cushion, squeezing an imaginary cushion, etc.
➤ Link some of these movements together to create a phrase.
➤ Vary the speed, size and level of the movements.

How does the cushion feel?
➤ Soft, furry, squishy. Explore each word using movement, e.g. can you think of a movement for furry?

What does it look like?
➤ Bulging, square, furry, bright yellow. Explore each word using movement, e.g. a bulging movement, a square movement.

Activity 2
Using torches
➤ Working in low light using torches, choreograph the torch beams.
➤ How can you make the beams move? Jumping? Smoothly? Circling? Darting?

10

➤ Make the beams dance on different surfaces, e.g. ceiling, floor, walls, clothes, cloth.

Changing the light

Change the colour and level of the light in your space (use different coloured light bulbs, stage lighting with coloured gels).

➤ How does this colour make people feel? Can you find movements to show this?

➤ What about when the colour is brighter and stronger? Or lower and fainter?

➤ Link movement ideas together to form phrases.

➤ Vary phrases by altering the speed, size, length, dynamics and levels of movements.

Activity 3

Textures

➤ Introduce different textures to move over, e.g. bubble wrap, carpet tiles, sand, bark, screwed up paper bags.

➤ How does that feel? Can you show a movement to express that feeling?

➤ How do you want to move over the new texture? Crawl? Slide? Roll?

➤ Link movement ideas together to form phrases.

➤ Vary phrases by altering the speed, size, length, dynamics and levels of movements.

Activity 4

Surfaces

➤ Make the walls your main surface to work on, i.e. find ways of moving across a wall.

➤ Keep at least two different body parts in contact with the wall at any time, e.g. elbows and nose, back and hand, feet and hands.

➤ Devise a hands and feet dance, keeping them in contact with the wall at all times.

➤ Cover a wall in foil or another reflective material.

➤ How do you want to move? Try using the foil as a mirror – creating duets with reflections.

➤ Describe the foil. Can you find movements for those words?

10

Activity 5
Creating a smaller space

Use a parachute or another large piece of fabric to restrict the space.

➤ Working within in a small space, explore how your body can be comfortable, e.g. crouched, lying, sitting.

➤ Explore some small movements, and body shapes.

➤ How can you travel around this small space?

➤ Link some of these ideas together.

Activity 6
Using a different space as a dance space

➤ Have you danced outside? Rounders, netball or football pitch, bike shed, courtyard.

➤ Have you danced in other inside spaces? Corridors, dining room, reception, pools?

➤ How does the new space make you feel?

➤ What do you want to do there? For example, slide down corridors, dodge between dinner tables.

➤ Are there lines, pathways, boundaries or any shapes to trace and explore? For example, balancing on, travelling on or across, dodging around.

➤ When the space is being used normally, how does it feel? For example, busy – find a movement to show 'busy'. Now find another 'busy' movement, using a different body part.

➤ How would you like the space to feel? For example, gentle, serene, full of action, bursting with energy. Find a movement to show these.

Groundworks: an outdoor site-specific choreographic performance

10

107

Remember

➤ Get any electrical/lighting changes checked for health and safety.
➤ If working underneath a parachute or other material, it can get very hot.
➤ Check that spaces are safe.
➤ Get permission to use an alternative space.
➤ Check safety of floor surfaces for feet, wheels, frames, etc. especially if covering with another surface.

Dance/choreographic skills involved

➤ Exploration of movements
➤ Spatial awareness
➤ Reacting to a variety of stimuli
➤ Improvisation
➤ Exploring movement ideas

Personal/group skills involved

➤ Improvising
➤ Using a range of stimuli
➤ Group negotiation
➤ Working individually
➤ Decision-making

Individual/partner work

Equipment needed: good quality children's bubbles, cloth or mop for clearing any bubble solution from floor

Activity 1
One person blows bubbles while others watch how the bubbles move.
➤ Using one body part, copy the movement dynamic of the bubbles, e.g. slow, gentle, descending, floating, smooth, light.
➤ Describe (in words or in movement) *how* the bubbles move – the movement dynamic, speed, etc.
➤ Describe (in words or in movement) *where* the bubbles move – the pathway.
➤ Explore what other body parts you can use to trace the journey of a slow, gently descending bubble, e.g. lying on your back using your feet, nose, shoulder.
➤ Working in pairs, mirror (copy) your partner. Try including physical contact, e.g. shoulders physically touching and descending gently.

Activity 2
Work in pairs, taking it in turns to blow the bubbles. One person blows bubbles high into the air, and the other has to pop them.
➤ Experiment using different body parts to pop bubbles, e.g. shoulder, foot, back of head, back.
➤ Vary the levels that you pop the bubbles, e.g. high level with foot, low level with shoulder.

Using bubbles as a stimulus

Activity 3
Remove the bubbles. The dancers choreograph phrases to build a dance based on their movements popping bubbles.
➤ Pairs identify and select two or more of their favourite positions for popping bubbles.
➤ The partners mirror each other's positions, or devise a position to contrast with their partner's position.

10

109

> *Example*
> Dancer 1 is popping an imaginary bubble with her shoulder at a low level. Dancer 2 sits or stands as tall as possible, popping an imaginary bubble up high with his head.

➤ Link the positions together using turns or jumps.
➤ Vary the speed of the linking movements.
➤ Restrict the space – the dancers perform as close together as possible without any physical contact.
➤ Develop your positions to include physical contact, so that in each position the two dancers are physically connected – shoulder and leg, head and back.

Different music will encourage different dynamics. Experiment with different types. Ask dancers to watch each other and notice the differences.

Remember
➤ Bubble solution can sting eyes – so avoid contact with faces.
➤ Bubble solution can make floor surfaces slippery.
➤ Some students may have medical conditions and physical management programmes that do not allow physical contact.

Dance/choreographic skills involved
➤ Improvisation
➤ Spatial awareness
➤ Awareness of body parts
➤ Exploring different levels and different speeds
➤ Selecting, ordering and developing phrases
➤ Partner work – duets
➤ Movement memory

Personal/group skills involved
➤ Decision making
➤ Partner work
➤ Co-operation
➤ Imagination
➤ Creativity
➤ Memory
➤ Awareness of body parts
➤ Spatial awareness

Group or pair work

Equipment needed: different lengths of elastic sewn into loops

Activity 1

Work in a large group for this activity.

➤ Standing in a circle, everyone holds a piece of elastic.
➤ Experiment with movements:
  ➤ finding different ways of stretching the elastic,
  ➤ using different body parts to hold the elastic, e.g. elbow (in crook), feet, behind backs, behind knees,
  ➤ finding different ways of moving the elastic, e.g. up and down, side to side, inwards and outwards, wiggling, flicking, slapping, feeding it through legs.
➤ Each dancer can contribute a movement idea for everyone to copy.
➤ Encourage dancers to observe and copy the movements carefully, noticing the speed, rhythm, level (high, medium, low), size and exact detail of the movement itself.
➤ Each dancer can choose four favourite movements, order them in a sequence and practise them. These can form the basis of a circle dance using the elastic.

A whole group using one elastic

Developing movements

➤ Vary the levels used: work seated, lying on the floor on back or stomach, standing, crouching.
➤ Vary the speed, size and rhythm of the movements.
➤ Combine an established phrase with other tasks, such as travelling as a group at a low level, turning the elastic so that it is at a higher level than any dancer.

Different music will encourage different types of movement responses. Experiment with a variety of music styles, cultures and combinations of instruments, and instruments/voice.

Finding different ways of moving and holding the elastic

Elastics can be used to define an area within a larger space. Such an area can be used for:

10

➤ sharing and showing ideas/work,

➤ a specific activity – balancing, still positions, jumping,

➤ time out.

Activity 2

Work in pairs for this activity.

➤ Pairs can experiment with the movements that can be made with different lengths of elastic.

➤ Link and develop the phrases as above for circle dances.

➤ Introduce themes, such as being close together, being as far apart and as contrasting as possible to your partner, but still holding the elastic.

Activity 3

Work in pairs for this activity.

Problem solving

Use your bodies to get the elastic into a mess, muddle, knots by:

➤ climbing in and out of it,

➤ weaving around each other,

➤ taking the elastic under and over itself.

Then reverse the process to un-muddle it!

Shape making

➤ Move to create a series of elastic shapes, e.g. oblongs and triangles.

➤ Use different body parts to create stretched shapes on different levels, e.g. feet standing on one end of the elastic, stretched arms holding the other.

Activity 4

Work in a group of three for this activity.

Weight taking

➤ Two dancers hold the elastic taut either side of the third dancer.

➤ The third dancer leans backwards or sideways into the elastic.

➤ The other two control the tightness of the elastic, moving it backwards until the leaning member of the group is off balance and is being held by the elastic. As trust and skill builds, the speed and size of the lean can be increased.

Remember

➤ Elastic is very 'ping-able' and can potentially be flicked at people. Ensure that activities are exciting and enjoyable enough to engage all participants positively.

➤ Small movements and moments of stillness are valuable contributions.

➤ Enthusiastic movements by one dancer will have a physical impact on those either side, e.g. people being pulled and wrenched by big, unexpected movements.

➤ Care must be taken to ensure that the third dancer is well supported in the weight-taking activity.

➤ If physical contact is involved, check that all the dancers' physical management programmes include this.

➤ Some medical conditions may prohibit sudden physical contact – seek advice.

➤ Care is needed and all dancers must be aware of how to make physical contact carefully and safely.

Dance/choreographic skills involved

➤ Improvisation
➤ Exploration of movement ideas
➤ Working at a variety of levels and speeds
➤ Exploring movement dynamics (quality of movement)
➤ Pair and group work
➤ Selecting, ordering and developing phrases
➤ Movement memory
➤ Observation skills

Personal/group skills involved

➤ Decision making
➤ Imagination
➤ Improvisation
➤ Memory
➤ Working with a prop
➤ Working as part of a group
➤ Partner work
➤ Co-operation
➤ Contributing ideas

10

113

Relaxing
Passing a ball/balloon

Group activity

Equipment needed: balls, hoops, beanbags, etc.

Activity
➤ With the group sitting, lying or standing in a circle, one person starts by passing a ball to the person next to them.
➤ That person then passes it on to the person next to them, and so on until it has been passed all the way round the circle.
➤ Vary the levels that the ball is passed at, e.g. high then low then high…
➤ Make the person next to you reach, twist, bend, or curl for the ball, e.g. by holding the ball high or low or behind them.
➤ Develop movements by asking for other variations, such as high, twisting, low, through a body part (e.g. legs or under arm).
➤ Specify that hands cannot be used to pass the object. Experiment and try elbows, feet, knees, etc.

Passing a balloon

Vary the task
➤ The person about to receive the ball makes an interesting still shape using their whole body.
➤ The person passing the ball rolls the ball on and across the receiver's body shape and then leaves the ball at the body part they want the person to receive the ball e.g. crook of an arm, between feet, etc.

Working in pairs

Vary the prop
➤ Use different sorts of props, as appropriate, e.g. bean bags, marble, hoop.
➤ Pass an invisible something around the group, using hands or another body part.
➤ Try something alive and wriggly, something heavy, something precious.
➤ Pass a physical sensation around the circle, e.g. a pat on the head, hand squeeze, drumming fingers on shoulders, squeeze on the shoulder.
➤ Try passing a rub on the back, while everyone has their eyes closed.

A whole group passing a pat on the head

10

Notice the 'physical listening' and anticipation that takes place, as everyone concentrates on 'feeling' the movement.

Encourage participants to work non-verbally and avoid verbal planning.

Remember
➤ Props used need to be accessible to all participants. Be aware e.g. if particularly fine motor skills are needed to handle a specific object.
➤ This activity requires people to be comfortable about touching, and being touched by someone else.
➤ If physical contact is involved, check that all the dancers' physical management programmes include this.
➤ Some medical conditions may prohibit sudden physical contact – seek advice.
➤ Care is needed and all dancers must be aware of how to make physical contact carefully and safely.

Dance/choreographic skills involved
➤ Improvising
➤ Exploring body parts
➤ Exploring use of levels
➤ Exploring different movement dynamics
➤ Imagination
➤ Kinaesthetic skills (feeling a movement, e.g. working with eyes closed)
➤ Working non-verbally

Personal/group skills involved
➤ Working within a group
➤ Non verbal negotiation
➤ Imagination
➤ Improvising
➤ Physical contact
➤ Problem solving

10

Relaxing
Paint brushes

Pair activity

Equipment needed: paint brushes – different thicknesses and types of bristles

Activity

➤ One person in each pair sits, lies or stands in a way that he or she finds very comfortable and relaxing.

➤ The pair negotiate and agree which body part is going to be used as the surface – e.g. backs of hands, arms, neck – or the leader can state the surface to be used.

➤ The person who is 'doing' uses paint brushes to create different sensations on their partner's body surface, e.g hand, arm, back, leg. *Important: the person who is having the activity done to them, should always have the option of stopping the activity.*

➤ Use different types of brush, e.g. different thicknesses, types of bristle, or roll the wooden handle across the body surface.

➤ Vary the movement, e.g. stroking, stippling, dabbing, whisking, rolling, flicking.

➤ Vary the dynamic and speed, e.g. light touch, heavy touch, fast, slow, increasing pace and pressure, decreasing the pressure (heavy to soft).

➤ Vary the patterns you are tracing, e.g. zigzags, spots, circles, crosses, meandering lines, spirals, letters, numbers.

➤ Swop roles so that the person 'doing' now relaxes and has the activity done to them.

Non-verbal feedback
Encourage the dancers to work non-verbally.

The people 'doing' should watch and feel their partner's physical response to different types of touch and stop if their partner seems uncomfortable in any way.

Physical responses will vary and may include:
➤ stiffening
➤ tensing

10

➤ withdrawing body part
➤ relaxing
➤ fidgeting
➤ giggling
➤ giving more weight to partner, e.g. really relaxing a hand and letting the partner totally support the weight of it.

Remember
➤ If you use music to accompany this exercise, your choice will influence the quality of touch used. Choose your music carefully.
➤ If a student has no movement in the hands, and therefore cannot manipulate the paintbrushes, they can direct someone else to carry out the activity on their partner, indicating how, where and which brushes should be used.
➤ Non-verbal feedback must be constantly monitored to ensure that dancers are aware and responsive to their partner.

Dance/choreographic skills involved
➤ Use of speed
➤ Use of dynamics
➤ Working in pairs
➤ Relaxing body

Personal/group skills involved
➤ Receiving careful touch
➤ Giving careful touch
➤ Decision-making
➤ Working in pairs
➤ Being aware of others' feelings
➤ Relaxing
➤ Trusting partner

Relaxing Stuck

Pairs activity

Equipment needed: none

Activity

➤ Working in pairs, choose a body part (or the leader can specify) e.g. wrists, foreheads, backs.

➤ Partners then have to improvise (moving without talking or planning), keeping those body parts physically touching each other wherever they move. If needed each pair can identify a leader, and a follower, taking turns to take each role so that both experience leading and following. Eventually the dancers will be able to negotiate leading and following non-verbally, without planning 'turns'.

➤ Encourage the dancers to work non-verbally, physically listening, feeling and responding to the change of directions, speed and dynamic of movements.

Choosing a body part

Encourage dancers to vary their movements by:

➤ finding the biggest stretch they can manage,

➤ finding a way of turning together,

➤ working at floor level or as low as possible,

➤ exploring different movement dynamics, e.g. gentle, continuous, smooth, never-ending, jagged, broken, sharp.

Encourage dancers to build phrases by:

➤ repeating and linking two or three movements together and finishing in a particular way, e.g. at low level.
➤ choosing three different body parts and building a phrase, e.g. two movements where heads are touching, a way of turning with heads touching, two movements with backs touching, a way of travelling together, two movements with feet touching.

Remember

➤ This activity requires people to be comfortable about touching, and being touched by someone else.
➤ If physical contact is involved, check that all the dancers' physical management programmes include this.
➤ Some medical conditions may prohibit sudden physical contact – seek advice.
➤ Care is needed and all dancers must be aware of how to make physical contact carefully and safely.
➤ Encourage participants to move slowly and carefully as they get used to the activity and their partner.
➤ Small movements are just as valid as larger ones.

Dance/choreographic skills involved

➤ Working with a partner – duet
➤ Improvising
➤ Working with given restrictions
➤ Exploring a variety of levels
➤ Exploring movement vocabulary
➤ Body awareness
➤ Spatial awareness

Personal/group skills involved

➤ Working non-verbally
➤ Non-verbal negotiation
➤ Improvising
➤ Working with a partner
➤ Physical contact
➤ Decision making

10

Movement words

Words that describe movement can be used:

➤ as a basis for a creative task, e.g. create a movement for each of these words – stretch, fall, spin. This leads to a basic movement phrase that can then be developed in different ways.

➤ to describe what you see when you watch others dancing.

➤ to encourage dancers to be specific and articulate when suggesting or describing movements, e.g. What kind of a turn? Spinning, twizzle, whisking, etc.

These movement words may stimulate ideas for creative tasks, or be the beginning of a list that the group can add to, in order to expand your collective movement/dance vocabulary.

TURN	**TWIST**	REVOLVE		STRETCH	
dodge	**SWIRL**	*SPIN*	**TWIRL**	EXPaND	dart
cut	*SWIVEL*	TWISSLE	SPIRAL		REACH
swerve	EXTEND	ENLARGE		flit	dash
scurry	whiz	rush	zip	race	**tear**	dart
weave	**DODGE**	Lunge	*plunge*		pounce
grab	swipe	swoop	duck		jittery
jumpy	edgy	GROW	*hover*	plunge	**float**
drift	**EMERGE**	slump	broken	*jerky*	pointy
sharp	**uneven**	soar	ASCEND	**crash**	INCREASE
Sustained	**ongoing**	continuous		**endless**	RISE
poise	steadiness	***calm***	peaceful	relaxed

Further reading

Dance Ideas – Kate Harrison, John Auty
Hodder & Stoughton Ltd, 1991
ISBN 0 340 42770 1

Hopping Home Backwards – Penny Greenland
JABADAO, 18 Branch Rd, Armley, Leeds LS12 3AQ, 2000
ISBN 1 903819 01 6

Making an Entrance – Adam Benjamin
Routledge, 2001
ISBN 0 415 25144 3

Making Dance Special – Melanie Peter
David Fulton Publishers Ltd, 1997
ISBN 1 85346 434 1

Useful addresses

Arts Council of England
14 Great Peter St
London
SW1P 3NQ
Tel: 020 7333 0100

Scottish Arts Council
12 Manor Place
Edinburgh
EH3 7DD
Tel: 0131 226 6051

Arts Council of Wales
Museum Place
Cardiff
CF1 3NX
Tel: 029 2037 6500

Contact the Arts Councils for information on regional/national dance contacts, e.g. National Dance Agencies, Dance Companies, Arts & Disability/Disability Arts Organisations, practitioners and projects

Incite ARTS
7 Bishops Rd
Sutton Coldfield
West Midlands
B73 6HX
Tel: 0121 686 7300

Dance and combined arts: Projects, training, etc. Focus on inclusion

Foundation for Community Dance
Cathedral Chambers
2 Peacock Lane
Leicester
LE1 5PX
Tel: 0116 251 0516

Community dance: Artists' directory, courses, conferences, publications.

JABADAO

18 Branch Road
Armley
Leeds
LS1 3AQ
Tel: 0113 231 0650

Dance and movement: Courses, resources, publications, projects, etc.

National Dance Teachers' Association

29 Larkspur Ave
Burntwood
Staffordshire
WS7 8SR
Tel: 01543 685 162

Dance in education: Courses, quarterly publications, etc.

Glossary

Canon	dancers performing the same movement/phrases with staggered starting times, so an overlap is created
Choreographic device	a tool that can be used when making dances, i.e. using canon
Connecting	making contact with
Dynamics	the way a movement is danced, the quality and energy of a movement including time, space, weight, force
Echoing	repeating, this may not necessarily be repetition of exactly the same movement but it will be recognisable
Improvisation	unplanned exploration, composing as you go
Kinaesthetic experience	feeling the sensations of movements, e.g. sensing through the body
Mirroring	copying, as if a mirror image
Non-verbal	without using spoken words
Pace	rate of speed and timing
Physical listening	allowing your body to be aware of any movement and/or sense of feeling, e.g. hesitancy, anxiety, excitement
Picking up on responses	being open to and acting on any reactions (verbal or physical) shown
Reflecting	echoing, sending back
Spatial terms	words and terminology that refer to the use of space within dance
Unison	dancers performing the same movement at the same time

© Questions Publishing Company